BUNGALOW KITCHENS

BUNGALOW KITCHENS

by Jane Powell

with photographs by Linda Svendsen

GIBBS·SMITH
P
PUBLISHER

Salt Lake City

TITLE PAGE: RESEMBLING FURNITURE MORE THAN UTILITARIAN STORAGE, CABINETS IN THE BUTLER'S PANTRY OF THE GAMBLE HOUSE HAVE GLASS DOORS THAT SLIDE ON WOODEN TRACKS. THE LIGHT FIXTURE HANGS FROM A DECORATIVE WOODEN CEILING CANOPY.

First Edition
04 03 02 01 00 5 4 3 2 1

Text copyright © 2000 by Jane Powell
Photographs copyright © 2000 by Linda Svendsen

Published by
Gibbs Smith, Publisher
P.O. Box 667
Layton, Utah 84041

Orders: (1-800) 748-5439
E-mail: info@gibbs-smith.com
Website: www.gibbs-smith.com

Edited by Suzanne Taylor
Designed and produced by Traci O'Very Covey, Salt Lake City
Printed and bound in Hong Kong

Library of Congress Cataloging-in-Publication Data
Powell, Jane, 1952-
        Bungalow kitchens / Jane Powell; photographs by
    Linda Svendsen.
        p. cm.
    ISBN 0-87905-950-8
    1. Kitchens—United States—History—20th
    century. I. Title.

TX653.P69 2000
643'.3'09730904—dc21   99-053493

Contents

This 1915 kitchen at Ardenwood Historic Farm in Fremont, California, has been preserved in its original state. Though it may look old-fashioned, it functions very much like a modern kitchen, laid out in an L shape with an island. An icebox refrigerator is at the end of a run of cabinets; the stove is at the other end. Not shown in the photo is a Hoosier cabinet against the left-hand wall. Windows on two sides provide daylight and ventilation. Both electric light and a kerosene lamp are provided since this was a farm and early electric power was not reliable. Much of the vintage kitchen equipment, including a cherry pitter, apple peeler, bottle stopper, coffee grinder, and some early electric toasters (on the open shelves), is still in use as part of the farm's educational programs.

Acknowledgments

There are many people and organizations without whom this book would not have been possible. I would first like to thank Linda Svendsen, for her beautiful photography and for indulging my obsession with vintage linoleum. Next I would like to thank the homeowners, who welcomed us into their kitchens: Steve Austin and Cathy Hitchcock, Barbara Babcock, Stephanie Bailey, Susan and Stephen Booth, George Bramson, Anthony Bruce, Marilyn and George Brumder, Ann and Andre Chaves, Paul Courtwright and J. Wade Williams, Kim and Rob Covey, Leslie Emmington, Norman Finnance and Mike Reandeau, Lyn Fountain, Loretta and Gary Graham, Jackie and Bob Gustafson, Mr. and Mrs. Jared Haight, Julie Hardgrove and Cliff Cline, Joann and Don Hausler, Cathy Hitchcock and Steve Austin, Mick Hollis, Molly and Duane McDade-Hood, Karen Jacques and Ken Wilcox, Lina and Wayne Knowles, Deborah and Alan Kropp, Phaedra and Mark Ledbetter, Michelle and Chris Lehman, Lori and Jeffrey Leonard, Roy Little and Jim Raidl, Betsy Martin and Rai Peterson, Heidi Mollenhauer and Kirk Wise, Sian Oblak and Charlie Ma, Jobie and Patrick O'Neil, Leticia and Rene Perez, Suzanne and Steven Roth, Don Shelman and Bill Jolliffe, Marilyn Thomas and Jim Bixler, Vreni and Jerry Watt, Ron Webber and Bill Pfeifer, Wanda Westberg and Richard Pettler, Carole Bess White, Larry Willits, Kathy and Art Zeigler. Thanks also to Fran Bartosek at Ardenwood Historic Farm (Patterson House); Lynda Guthrie and Theresa Wilkins at Dunsmuir House; Judy Benda, Ted Bosley, Joann Lynch, and Bobbi Mapstone at the Gamble House; and Melissa Patton at the Lanterman House.

We would never have found all these kitchens without referrals from the following: Fred Albert at Seattle Homes and Lifestyles; Tim Hansen and Dianne Ayres; Steven Ballew at the Sacramento Bungalow Heritage Association; Su Bacon at Historic Lighting; Ted Bosley at the Gamble House; Anthony Bruce at Berkeley Architectural Heritage Association; Brian Coleman; Lynne and Audel Davis; Paul Duchscherer; Erik Hanson; Larry Kreisman at Historic Seattle; Christopher Molinar at the Gamble House Bookstore; Mark Novakowski; Pasadena Heritage; Mary Ellen Polson at *Old House Journal*; Ron Reuter; Tom Shess at *North Park News*; Neal Skibinski; Save Our Heritage Organization (San Diego); Dale Slusser and David Greene at the Bosco-Milligan Foundation (Portland); and Laurie Taylor at Ivy Hill Interiors. I apologize if I have forgotten anyone.

Many people contributed knowledge and/or access to period books and magazines, including Dianne Ayres and Tim Hansen, Erik Hanson, and Riley Doty. I am especially grateful to Riley Doty and Royal Yates for information about tile; Steven Ballew for finding a source for porcelain-enameled metal counters; Mary Ellen Polson for recommending books; Margaret Mair at the Stowe Center; Rose Braunzak at Armstrong Floors for period advertisements; Madeline Innes at Rejuvenation Lamp and Fixture for providing photographs of light fixtures; and Randy Hunter for period advertising.

I am grateful to my many friends and acquaintances in the Arts & Crafts Community—Arts & Crafts people are just the best! I'd also like to thank my fellow board members at the Oakland Heritage Alliance for their patience this last year with my prolonged photo-shooting absences and general distractedness as well as for their support.

The book would not be what it is without the fabulous illustrations by Betsy Martin, and I must also thank Jeanette Sayre for her assistance with the book proposal, as well as her continuing advice on all matters aesthetic and otherwise. Doug Keister provided invaluable advice concerning various business aspects. And I would never have written the book at all without the encouragement, support, and friendship of Bruce Smith and Paul Duchscherer. And, of course, I must thank my editor, Suzanne Taylor, for cleaning up my words but leaving their spirit intact and for leaving in most of the puns.

Last but not least, I want to thank my parents, Nelson and Peg Powell, and my two sisters, Mary Enderle and Nancy Klapak. From them I learned the important things in life: love, friendship, laughter, learning, and food. All these things are best served in the kitchen. I also learned from them that family is not just about relatives, and I am grateful to have an extended family, not only of aunts, uncles, and cousins, but also a family of friends. To me, their friendship is beyond price. And, of course, my life would not be complete without my feline companions: Milo, Ubu, Emma, and Zoe. A bungalow requires cats, and possibly cats require a bungalow.

JANE POWELL

Introduction

Almost anyone knows how to create an attractive living room but to work out a kitchen which is equally a "winner" is a far more unique achievement. EMILY BURBANK, *Be Your Own Decorator*, 1924 A couple of years ago at the Craftsman Weekend in Pasadena, I attended a lecture about kitchens by Gordon Bock, editor of the *Old House Journal*. It was an interesting talk about

THE FACE FRAMES OF THE CABINETS IN THIS KITCHEN ECHO THE PEGGED DETAIL OF THE DOOR CASINGS, AND THE BEAD-BOARD CENTER PANELS TIE IN WITH THE WAINSCOTING. THE MUNTINS ON THE GLASS CABINET DOORS MATCH THE WINDOWS IN THE HOUSE. THESE CABINETS WERE BUILT BY THE HOMEOWNER USING (APPROPRIATELY) A CRAFTSMAN TABLE SAW. AN UNUSUAL COPPER BACKSPLASH SITS BEHIND THE SINK. A GE MONITOR-TOP REFRIGERATOR, A VINTAGE ELECTRIC STOVE (NOT SHOWN), AND A COLLECTION OF VINTAGE PACKAGING AND KITCHENWARE GIVE THE KITCHEN AN AUTHENTIC LOOK.

how the introduction of new technologies and materials had changed the design and function of kitchens in the early twentieth century. At the end of the lecture, people were asking specific questions about where to buy certain items, how to do things, how to fit the latest technology into an old kitchen, and Gordon, to his credit, did his best to answer them. But it became clear to me that people were looking for much more detailed information. And I realized that after twelve years of living in, researching, and fixing up bungalows, I had accumulated that information. That is when I decided to write this book.

This isn't so much a "how-to" book as a "what-to" book. It lays out what there was, when it was available, and how it went together. Both obsessive restoration and compromise solutions are explored for each element, allowing you to decide where you fall on that continuum in regard to each item.

I am making a few assumptions. First of all, I'm assuming that you have already seen enough other kitchen books or magazines to have a working knowledge of the basic concepts: the work triangle, standard layouts (galley, U-shaped, L-shaped, island), the difference between stock, semi-custom, and custom cabinets; some information about contractors and contracts, the role of architects and kitchen designers; and the various materials that are available. This is important basic knowledge for any type of kitchen.

Although this book is called *Bungalow Kitchens*, these kitchens were not found exclusively in bungalows. They were found in any style of house from about 1890 until World War II. Late Victorians and Edwardians, Colonial Revivals, Prairie houses, Arts & Crafts houses, Tudors, Spanish and other romantic revivals, Art Deco and Moderne houses—all had similar kitchens.

Many people have asked me where I acquired all this arcane knowledge about period kitchens. Although I have done a lot of research in old books and magazines as well as contemporary publications, the truth is I learned most of it by observation. In my work, I buy run-down Arts & Crafts houses, which I restore and then sell. In the course of this, I have seen hundreds of old houses and many original or partly original kitchens. I paid attention, and patterns and similarities

began to emerge. I have restored a few kitchens that were original, built new period kitchens from scratch, and even turned a 1960s kitchen into a period kitchen. I learned a lot by doing it myself; I learned a lot more from my mistakes. I wrote this book so the learning curve wouldn't be quite so steep for others.

The kitchen was and is the most complex room in the house. The demands placed on it at the turn of the twentieth century are nothing compared to the demands placed on it now. Then it was essentially a workroom, a utilitarian space, yet far more complicated than the rest of the house. It is still fundamentally a workroom, but we have very different expectations. Not only must it be functional, now it is seen as a gathering place for family and guests, a status symbol, a place for projects, and a vehicle for self-expression. During the Arts & Crafts movement, it was believed that family life would center in the living room around the hearth. The kitchen has now supplanted the living room as the central place in our homes.

As expectations of kitchens increased throughout the twentieth century, most original kitchens were either ripped out or modernized. The kitchen is the room least likely to be intact in an old house. In our consumer society, there is continual pressure to modernize, to have the newest thing, to be fashionable. Remember, it was American corporations that invented "planned obsolescence." Many perfectly functional old kitchens were replaced with the latest trendy designs of a particular decade by homeowners who wanted to be "modern," with the encouragement of various people who stood to make money from the project. As these houses were rediscovered toward the end of the century, much time and energy was put into restoring the exteriors, the formal rooms, and even the bathrooms to a period style. Walking through a faithfully restored living room and dining room into a kitchen from a much later decade gives one cognitive dissonance. Of course, until now, very little information on period kitchens has been available.

Have nothing in your houses that you do not know to be useful, or believe to be beautiful.

—WILLIAM MORRIS

An early-twentieth-century kitchen could be described as *utilitarian*. Somewhere along the way this became a derogatory term. We apparently no longer value simplicity or usefulness as virtues. Yet simplicity and usefulness, honesty of design and materials were central themes of the Arts & Crafts movement. There is nothing inherently wrong with utility; indeed, the Shakers made useful objects of great beauty and simplicity. It is true that much useful technology came about in the twentieth century, but we also seem very enamored with "bells and whistles" for which we have no real use. Thousands, probably hundreds of thousands of perfectly functional period kitchens have been ripped out and replaced with the day's state-of-the-art kitchens. Perhaps you have one: plywood cabinets and gold-flecked laminate from the sixties, an avocado-and-harvest-gold nightmare from the seventies, a mauve, teal, and black "contemporary" kitchen from the eighties? Now those kitchens just look dated. A period kitchen, on the other hand, looks right. In an old house, it appears timeless, not dated. It belongs there.

There are many reasons to have a period kitchen, to either restore the one that is there or build a new one in a period way. An original kitchen is rare and should be preserved. For the most part, these kitchens are not even documented or protected in any way except by caring homeowners. Yet they are an important piece of history: the history of the house, the history of the twentieth century, the history of women, the history of technology. They can

easily be made to function for the twenty-first century without compromising their integrity. The craftsmanship and now irreplaceable resources that went into them should not be lightly discarded. Even a modest bungalow was built with old-growth lumber of a quality that is difficult to find nowadays, and we can no longer afford to send all those resources to the landfill just because we want to be fashionable. We are only caretakers of these houses and should not do anything that some subsequent owner will be cursing us for, as we may now be cursing whoever painted all the natural woodwork or replaced all the windows with cheap aluminum sliders. Imagine someone in 2075 exclaiming, "Look at those rainbow granite counters and recessed lights—must have been remodeled in the 1990s!"

A period kitchen will simplify your life. If you are building a new one or restoring an old one, the range of appropriate cabinets, hardware, and other elements is limited. This means far fewer decisions to make. A whole century of labor-saving devices do not seem to have given us any more free time. They have instead made life much more complex. It is time to choose the things that are actually helpful and jettison the merely novel (does anybody *need* a hot-dog cooker?). There is no need to have things that are overly fancy or that you don't use. Your kitchen should not be more impressive than your living room. If you want a kitchen with cabinets that resemble furniture, art-glass chandeliers, and marble floors, then please build a new house and put it there; leave the old houses alone. When making decisions about the kitchen in an old house, it is almost always better to make it simpler.

People often ask me about resale value, thinking that buyers expect the latest thing in kitchens, even in an old house. In my experience, buyers respond positively to period-style kitchens as long as they contain a dishwasher, disposal, frost-free refrigerator, functioning stove, and sufficient cabinet space. A period kitchen can have storage, counter space, a good work triangle, and all the other things that make a kitchen functional in modern terms while still looking like they belong in the house. And would you really want to sell your old house to buyers who wouldn't appreciate it?

They say that knowledge is power. Armed with the information in this book, you should be able to restore or re-create a period kitchen. And I hope you will.

History of the Modern Kitchen

The history of kitchens is in many ways the history of women. Since colonial times, the kitchen has been primarily the domain of women, either the woman of the house or female servants. The few men who cooked were chefs in restaurants. Well into the twentieth century, women had very little input into the design of the room where they spent most of their time and labor, and servants had no say at all. In the nineteenth century, kitchens were often found in the basement,

THIS BUTLER'S PANTRY FROM THE 1920s HAS TYPICAL CABINETS FOR STORAGE OF CHINA, FLATWARE, AND TABLE LINENS. BY THIS TIME, STORAGE AND STAGING OF FOOD BEFORE IT WENT TO THE DINING ROOM WERE THE PRIMARY FUNCTIONS; DISHWASHING HAD BEEN RELEGATED TO THE KITCHEN.

with little light, air, or ventilation. In middle- and upper-class homes, this was the domain of servants; therefore, little thought was given to making them comfortable or easing their workload. Servant girls from rural areas—later replaced by successive waves of immigrants, or blacks, in the case of the South—worked day and night with little time to themselves for rest or leisure. With the Industrial Revolution, many of the American-born servants opted for slightly better-paying jobs in factories, leaving their jobs to newly arrived immigrants—first the Irish, then the Eastern Europeans.

As it became more difficult to find servants, wages rose and the working conditions began to improve, some due to technological advances and some due to the lady of the house becoming more involved in running the kitchen. Previously, the idealized Victorian woman had time for socializing, improving her mind, raising her children, and doing charitable work, living a lifestyle only through the backbreaking labor of others. As the nineteenth century

progressed, even the immigrant women began to take jobs in factories, where the working conditions were not much better, but where they at least had some chance to socialize with coworkers. This led to much difficulty in attracting servants, so women reluctantly began to take on a greater role in the kitchen, then began to complain about the drudgery of housekeeping, much of which was true and still is. This changing of the guard also led to the publication of numerous household manuals and receipt (recipe) books with advice about the various aspects of running a household and a lot of moralizing and propaganda about the nobleness of it. The most influential of these were written by Catherine Beecher, including *A*

THE KITCHEN OF THE HARRIET BEECHER STOWE HOUSE IN HARTFORD, CONNECTICUT, SHOWS SOME OF THE INNOVATIVE IDEAS PROPOSED BY HER SISTER CATHERINE, INCLUDING OPEN SHELVING, GROOVED DRAINBOARD, AND DRAWERS UNDER THE SINK FOR STORAGE. (PHOTO COURTESY HARRIET BEECHER STOWE CENTER)

IN THIS CIRCA 1908 KITCHEN BY ARCHITECTS GEORGE PLOWMAN AND JOHN HUDSON THOMAS, VERTICAL-GRAIN FIR CABINETS PROVIDE AMPLE STORAGE. A HIGH TILED WAINSCOT CONTINUES AROUND THE ROOM. IN ONE CORNER IS THE WORLD'S TINIEST BREAKFAST NOOK. (PLOWMAN ARCHIVES, UNIVERSITY OF OREGON)

Treatise on Domestic Economy for the Use of Young Ladies at Home and at School (1841*), Miss Beecher's Domestic Receipt Book* (1846), and her most influential work, *The American Woman's Home, or Principles of Domestic Science* (1869), co-authored with her sister Harriet Beecher Stowe. Later she also published *Miss Beecher's Housekeeper and Healthkeeper* and *The New Housekeeper's Manual* (1873).

Catherine Beecher may well be the mother of the modern kitchen. It was she who first proposed such concepts as storing foodstuffs near where they would be used; different preparation areas for different foods; bins for flour, meal, and such; the broom closet, open shelving, and other custom storage; and it is believed by many that she was the first to propose grooved drain boards next to the sink. She also espoused doing things systematically to save time and energy:

A full supply of all conveniences in the kitchen and cel-

lar, and a place appointed for each article, very much facilitates domestic labor. It would be far better for a lady to give up some expensive article in the parlor, and apply the money thus saved to kitchen conveniences, than to have a stinted supply where the most labor is to be performed. Expensive mirrors and pier-tables in the parlor, and an unpainted, gloomy, ill-furnished kitchen, not infrequently are found under the same roof.

An early and enthusiastic supporter of cookstoves, she wrote about a particular stove:

. . . although it is so complicated in its various contrivances as to demand intelligent management in order to secure all its advantages, it also can be used satisfactorily even when the mistress and maid are equally careless and ignorant of its distinctive merits. To such it offers all the advantages of ordinary good stoves, and is extensively used by those who take no pains to understand and apply its peculiar advantages.

Beecher spent her life promoting the education of young women, and as the century progressed, others took up the cause; eventually studies in domestic science began to be offered at colleges and universities, leading to what became known as Home Economics. Others also built upon her pioneering work in the area of kitchens: cooking schools were established and numerous household manuals and cookbooks were published. One piece of advice from *The American Woman's Home* is still quite relevant:

It is equally important that young girls should be taught to do some species of handicraft that is generally done by men. To hang wallpaper, repair locks, glaze windows, and mend various household articles requires a skill in the use of tools which every young girl should acquire. If she never has any occasion to apply this knowledge and skill with her own hands, she will often find it needful in directing and superintending incompetent workmen.

The study of domestic science continued in the twentieth century. Although much of it was designed to convince women to stay in their assigned roles by making housekeeping seem as important as business, it still led to improvements in kitchen design and efficiency. The time-and-motion studies of Frank and Lillian Gilbreth and others led to the continuous countertop, standardized cabinet heights and depths, and the concept of the work triangle that we still use today.

The Arts & Crafts movement in the late nineteenth and early twentieth centuries had some influence on kitchen design, mostly in its call for sim-

I N THE BUTLER'S PANTRY OF THE GAMBLE HOUSE IN PASADENA, CHARLES AND HENRY GREENE DESIGNED EFFICIENT LAYOUT AND CABINETRY, AMPLE COUNTER SPACE, AND LARGE WINDOWS FOR LIGHT AND VENTILATION. THE PEGGED JOINTS AND OTHER CABINET DETAILS ARE A HALLMARK OF THE GREENE BROTHERS, WHOSE ATTENTION TO DETAIL EXTENDED EVEN TO THE UTILITARIAN PARTS OF THE HOUSE.

plification in all areas of life. An excerpt from Edward Carpenter's book *The Simplification of Life*, published in Gustav Stickley's *Craftsman* magazine in 1909, began by musing on Victorian excess:

No doubt immense simplifications of our daily life are possible; but this does not seem to be a matter which has been much studied. Rather hitherto the tendency has been all the other way, and every additional ornament to the

mantelpiece has been regarded as an acquisition and not as a nuisance; though one doesn't see any reason, in the nature of things, why it should be regarded as one more than the other. It cannot be too often remembered that every additional object in a house requires additional dusting, cleaning, repairing; and lucky you are if its requirements stop there. . . . If the desire for simplicity is not really present, no labor-saving appliances will make life simpler.

Stickley himself stated the following in regard to kitchens:

The very first requisites are that it should be large enough for comfort, well-ventilated and full of sunshine, and that the equipment for the work that is to be done should be ample, of good quality, and above all, intelligently selected. . . . In planning a house it should come in for the first thought instead of the last and its use as a din-

ing room as well as a kitchen should be carefully considered. . . . The properly planned kitchen should be as open as possible to prevent the accumulation of dirt. . . . Ample cupboard space for all china should be provided near the sink to do away with unnecessary handling, and the same cupboard, which should be an actual structural feature of the kitchen, should contain drawers for table linen, cutlery and smaller utensils, as well as a broad shelf which provides a convenient place for serving.

It is important to keep in mind that with the exception of such women as Catherine Beecher and the rare woman

A "MODERN" KITCHEN CIRCA 1920 IS NOT SO DIFFERENT FROM TODAY'S KITCHENS. THE LOWER CABINET DOORS HAVE UNUSUAL SURFACE-MOUNTED HINGES, AND THE UPPER CABINET TO THE RIGHT OF THE SINK IS A COOLER CABINET. THE LEFT-HAND CABINET HAS SHALLOW DRAWERS UNDERNEATH ITS GLASS DOORS.

architect like Julia Morgan, almost all kitchens in the late nineteenth and early twentieth centuries were designed and built by men. Since men did not cook they were not cognizant of what might be required. Things improved significantly in the twentieth century, although it was still hit or miss. Some architects, such as Charles and Henry Greene in Pasadena, showed remarkable sensitivity to effi-

THIS WOODBURNING 1915 WEDGEWOOD STOVE AT ARDENWOOD HISTORIC FARM IN FREMONT, CALIFORNIA, IS STILL BEING USED. NEXT TO IT SITS AN INSTANT WATER HEATER WITH BEAUTIFUL ART NOUVEAU DESIGNS IN THE CASTING. MANY OF THESE INSTANT HEATERS ARE STILL FUNCTIONING.

ciency, light, and ventilation in their kitchens, especially surprising since many of their commissions were for wealthy people whose kitchens would be used only by servants. The main difference between the kitchen of a modest bungalow and the kitchen of a wealthy home is likely to be its size and the existence of a butler's pantry, although butler's pantries were not unheard of in more modest homes. Some of the best kitchens were designed for the various plan-book and kit homes from such companies as Aladdin, Henry Wilson, and Sears Roebuck. Since most homes were small, much thought went into space-saving layouts and clever built-ins. Stock built-ins and kitchen cabinets could also be ordered from millwork companies and some of the companies that manufactured Hoosier cabinets. This allowed spec builders to install pre-built cabinets in different configurations rather than build cabinets in place. Of course, some spec builders were thoughtful and some were clueless. A kitchen from the first decade of the twentieth century is more likely to be a room containing a freestanding stove, wall-hung sink, worktable, and maybe one freestanding or built-in cabinet, with very little counter space (although this was not universally true). A kitchen from the 1920s is more likely to resemble what we think of as "modern": built-in cabinets, continuous countertops with tile-in sink, refrigerator in the kitchen instead of the utility porch, and possibly a breakfast room or nook. Kitchens are still being built by men, but at least now quite a few of them actually know how to cook. (Possibly this is what has led to the proliferation of such expensive kitchen toys as restaurant stoves, European appliances, and built-in refrigerators.)

Kitchens of the early twentieth century do not differ in significant ways from today's kitchens: we have new technology but the basic elements of stove, sink, refrigerator, and cabinets remain the same. A comparison of early-nineteenth-century kitchens with those from the turn of the twentieth century would be a different story. Huge advancements in technology and manufacturing led to radical changes in cooking, sanitation, lighting, food preservation, and even the role of women in society. These changes eventually resulted in the first modern kitchens.

Throughout the nineteenth century and well into the twentieth, there was a difference between urban and rural

The range at the 1899 Dunsmuir House in Oakland, California, burns wood, coal, or gas. Set on a glazed brick platform, the numerous ovens, large cooking area, and built-in hot-water tank were essential in the kitchen of this large estate. A large combination gas/electric light fixture hangs in the center of the room. Checkerboard linoleum would have been typical at the time, though this floor is from somewhat later.

kitchens. In rural areas, kitchens were at the center of family life, a gathering place for the family and any farmhands who worked for them. By contrast, in urban areas, the focus of family life and socializing was the dining room and parlor. Middle- and upper-class people rarely entered the kitchen except to instruct the servants. William Morris offered this observation: "In a country farm-house, the kitchen is uncommonly pleasant and home-like, the parlor dreary and useless." Naturally, advances in kitchen technology came first to urban areas and people with money, much later to rural areas.

At the beginning of the nineteenth century, Americans cooked over open fires or coals, in fireplaces, or in masonry ovens. Cookstoves were first manufactured in the 1820s, although they didn't really catch on until the 1850s. Since most people were used to hearth-cooking, many were intimidated by the new technology, which meant learning a whole new way to cook. Stoves originally burned wood,

but by the end of the nineteenth century, models that burned coal, oil, and gas were available. At first, there was a difference in terminology between a stove and a range: a range was built into a brick-lined enclosure (often the former fireplace), whereas a stove was freestanding. Later on the terms became interchangeable. Originally cast iron, stoves were later made of both cast iron and sheet metal. The Victorian and early-twentieth-century stoves could be quite ornate, with fancy casting and nickel-plated details, while later models from the 1920s to the 1940s became a

A TYPICAL OAK ICEBOX FROM 1915 AT ARDENWOOD HISTORIC FARM. THE DRIP PAN UNDERNEATH HAD TO BE EMPTIED REGULARLY. ON THE FLOOR NEXT TO IT IS AN ANTIQUE MOUSETRAP.

lot more streamlined. Stoves freed the cook somewhat from lifting the heavy iron pots necessary for hearth cooking, and lighter-weight cookware became available. Many stoves also had hot-water reservoirs or tanks attached to them, bringing a reliable and easy supply of hot water into the kitchen.

The next great kitchen advance, the basis of modern civilization, was the introduction of indoor plumbing in the 1870s. Urban areas installed citywide water and sewage systems as well as gas piping for lighting and stoves. The dry sink of the nineteenth century was replaced by a plumbed sink with separate hot and cold water taps. The importance of sewer systems cannot be overlooked either. Earlier in the nineteenth century, raw sewage often ran down the middle of the streets, and the drinking-water supply was often contaminated. People drank coffee or tea because the water had been boiled, or they drank beer or fermented cider because alcohol killed the bacteria. A growing awareness of germs and their relation to the spread of disease resulted not only in building municipal sewage systems but also in emphasizing hygiene and sanitation, which eventually bordered on obsession.

The third great kitchen advance was the advent of refrigeration and better storage methods for perishable foods. Ice chests became available in the 1860s, and by the turn of the twentieth century, iceboxes were extremely common. Electric refrigeration was used toward the end of the nineteenth century, although it did not become widespread until the 1920s. The terms *icebox* and *refrigerator* were used interchangeably. Before refrigeration, the primary methods for storing perishables were root cellars, springhouses (cooled by water), and canning, smoking, or drying. Although the first patent for what we now know as tin cans was procured in 1825, production of commercially canned and packaged goods was begun after the Civil War, at which time it expanded rapidly. Companies from that time, such as Heinz, Campbell's, Libby's, and Van Camp, are still in business. Many women continued to "put up" their own fruits, vegetables, and preserves even after the advent of packaged goods, but toward the end of the nineteenth century, the realization of the savings in time and effort represented by packaged foods caused sales to rise significantly.

The fourth great kitchen advance was the introduction of electricity. This led to better lighting, electric refrigeration, electric stoves, and a proliferation of labor-saving electric appliances. Many of the labor-saving devices were rather pointless, but that did not deter the manufacturers then any more than it does now. Initially, electrical outlets were few, resulting in housekeepers having to unscrew the lightbulb and screw in a plug adapter in order to plug in the various electric devices. But, as the twentieth century progressed, more outlets were added in addition to the lights.

Another influence on the development of the modern kitchen was scientific advancement in the areas of sanitation and hygiene. New discoveries about germs and their relation to disease led to an obsession with cleanliness. There was some merit in this devotion to sanitation. Vermin, insects, soot, and dust were common in an era of wood- and coal-burning stoves, gaslight, and unpaved streets. And before electric refrigeration, food spoilage was a serious problem. The laboratory-like white-tile-and-enamel "sanitary" kitchens of the first two decades of the twentieth century made it easy to see the dirt, insects, rodent droppings, or other threats to hygiene. It was thought that exposed plumbing would prevent germs

PACKAGED FOODSTUFFS, SHOWN HERE AT THE LANTERMAN HOUSE IN LA CAÑADA–FLINTRIDGE, WERE TIMESAVERS IN THE BUNGALOW ERA AND STILL FILL THAT ROLE TODAY.

resulting from dampness. In the 1920s and 1930s, many realized that a white kitchen was not the only solution, although plenty of all-white kitchens continued to be built. An article in *Pacific Coast Architect* in 1928 had this to say: "White tile and enamel were proclaimed as a panacea that righted all the evils to which kitchens of a past day were heir. Their use amounted to a religion. But, as a matter of fact, these measures produced results far from satisfactory." More color was introduced in the 1920s and 1930s, yet white continues to be popular as a kitchen color to the present time.

Since the number of servants decreased and some women began to enter the workforce, manufacturers responded not only with new labor-saving appliances but also with an ever-increasing variety of packaged foods. Canned foods were followed in the 1880s by the introduction of baking powder, in the 1890s by packaged cereals (Shredded Wheat and Grape-Nuts), commercially prepared soaps and scouring powders (Ivory and Sapolio), Kingsford's Corn

Starch, and at the turn of the century by Jell-O. By 1920 it was possible to purchase many products that we still use today: Campbell's Soups, Crisco, Nabisco Cookies and Crackers, Log Cabin Syrup, Borden's Condensed Milk, Heinz Ketchup and Vinegar, Van Camp's Pork and Beans, and Wesson Oil. In the late 1920s, Clarence Birdseye came up with a fast-freezing process for foods that had a significant impact on cooking and kitchens. Freezers became larger in order to store all the frozen foods, and eventually the two-door refrigerator-freezer that is now typical came into being.

Who knows what changes to the kitchen will take place in this century? There are those who predict that we will give up cooking entirely and take nutrition pills, that cook-ing will become an exotic ritual, almost like a religious observance. On the other hand, in a return to cooking meth-ods of previous centuries, there are people building open fireplaces in their kitchens in order to roast and cook over open flames. Others are eating fast food in their cars. In any case, a bungalow kitchen, with only a few modifications, can still fit easily into twenty-first-century life—and should.

Kitchens by Greene & Greene

Many period kitchens were designed by architects, yet most of them are not radically different from other kitchens of the time. A kitchen designed for a wealthy client might be larger, might have had electric refrigeration before it was common, and might have been better laid out, but the details generally were similar to the average builder's bungalow or plan-book house. The kitchens designed by Charles and Henry Greene of Pasadena were an exception. Their attention to detail and craftsmanship extended even to the utility areas of the houses they designed.

Charles and Henry Greene were born in 1868 and 1870, respectively, into a family that traced its lineage to Revolutionary War General Nathanael Greene on one side and Cotton Mather on the other. They spent their early childhood in Cincinnati and at their grandparents' farm in rural West Virginia. Their father moved the family to St. Louis while the boys were still in elementary school, and when it came time to send them to high school he chose the new Manual Training School of Washington University, the first of its kind in the country. He had already decided that his sons should be architects, and he felt the school would provide them with a good basis for architectural careers. There they spent half of each day on academic subjects, the other half on drawing, carpentry, metalwork, and other manual skills. After graduating, at their father's urging (and Charles was not too happy about it), they both enrolled in a two-year architecture program at MIT. After finishing the program, they both apprenticed at various Boston architectural firms. During this time, their parents moved west to Pasadena and were soon asking the boys to come for a visit. Upon arrival in 1893, the brothers found that Pasadena was not the cultural backwater they had feared, and within a few months they opened an architectural office downtown. Their first commissions were modest, but eventually they began to find wealthier clients, thus beginning the journey toward the architecture for which they are now known. Two of the modest houses, the Breiner house of 1894 and the Covelle house of 1895, greatly resemble side-gabled bungalows with dormers. By 1902 they had begun to design in the singular style that eventually led to the "ultimate bungalows" for which they are

CABINETS IN THE BUTLER'S PANTRY OF THE SPINKS HOUSE FEATURE PEGGED JOINTS, SEEN CLEARLY IN THE FOREGROUND. SIMPLE GLASS-PANELED DOORS SLIDE ON WOODEN TRACKS IN THE UPPER CABINETS. THE CEILING IN THIS SPACE IS QUITE LOW. A NICKEL SILVER SINK WITH AN ARCHED FAUCET SITS BENEATH A WINDOW. SHAPED WOODEN DRAWER HANDLES ARE VISIBLE AT LEFT.

LEFT TO RIGHT: THE INTERCOM PHONE AT THE ROBINSON HOUSE. ▪▪ A VIEW OF THE ORIGINAL ANNUNCIATOR/INTERCOM OF THE DUNCAN IRWIN HOUSE. THE TOP BOX HAS ARROWS SHOWING WHICH DOORBELL WAS BEING RUNG, AS THE HOUSE HAS SEVERAL DOORS. ▪▪ DETAIL OF THE JOINERY AT THE DEFOREST HOUSE.

famous. By 1905 they had begun their association with the brothers Peter and John Hall, who brought their exquisite craftsmanship to executing the Greenes' designs.

The kitchens they designed between 1905 and 1909 have many features in common with other kitchens of the period: stoves with hoods, iceboxes, wall-hung sinks, wooden floors, tiled walls, butler's pantries. The work areas are well thought out, but this is true of other kitchens as well. Where the Greene & Greene kitchens diverge is in the cabinetry and the attention to detail. The same kind of complex joinery and craftsmanship found in the more formal rooms is found in the kitchens (albeit in a simpler form and with less-exotic woods). Unlike the flat-panel cabinet doors found in most kitchens of the time, their doors are joined with battens and cloud-lifts or other motifs, sometimes with a decorative pattern of round-headed screws holding the battens to the boards underneath. The sides of the cabinets are joined to the fronts with decorative pegged joints. Even the outside ice-delivery door, while a common-enough feature in bungalow kitchens, is given a distinctive treatment.

This leads to questions about which one can only spec-ulate. Is this just part of the general obsessiveness of the Greenes or possibly of the Hall brothers, which also led them to chamfer the edges of basement support posts no one would ever see? Is it part of the holistic way in which they built, where all parts were important to the whole? Or had they actually given a lot of thought to kitchens and how to make them more livable and efficient? Certainly they would have been exposed to articles in architectural journals and other magazines about the subject. Did their experience at the Manual Training School give them some ideas about how to set up an efficient workroom, since a kitchen is essentially that? Did Charles, as the more artistic of the two, lobby for this part of the house to be as artistic as the rest? Did they give any more thought to the comfort and convenience of servants than the average gentleman, or did the decreased availability of household help have some impact on the design (not that most of their clients were doing their own cooking)? Certainly they hadn't given a whole lot of thought to the practical aspects of board-and-batten doors (difficult to clean), but then, they were men. A great deal more research will be needed to answer these questions, if indeed there are answers.

KITCHEN CABINETS IN THE 1909 GAMBLE HOUSE SHOW THE GREENES' ATTENTION TO DETAIL. ON THE UPPER CABINETS, THE FACE-FRAME JOINTS ARE PEGGED AND THE VERTICALS EXTEND ABOVE AND BELOW THE CABINET, WHERE THEY HAVE BEEN CAREFULLY ROUNDED OVER. ON THE LOWER CABINETS, WOODEN DRAWER HANDLES HAVE BEEN CAREFULLY SHAPED. THE CABINETS WERE BUILT IN PLACE, AS EVIDENCED BY THE SUBWAY TILE SEEN BEHIND THE GLASS DOORS.

CLOCKWISE FROM TOP: THE 1905 ROBINSON HOUSE BUTLER'S PANTRY FEATURES UPPER CABINETS WITH SIMPLE GLASS DOORS THAT LOCK, ALONG WITH LOWER BOARD-AND-BATTEN DOORS. THE UPPER CABINETS USE LOOPED CASEMENT HARDWARE, MORE OFTEN FOUND ON WINDOWS. AGAIN, THE FACE-FRAMES HAVE PEGGED JOINTS. ON THE LEFT IS A BUILT-IN ICEBOX SURROUNDED BY WOOD TRIM. THE WOODEN COUNTERTOP HAS BEEN PAINTED. THIS PHOTO WAS TAKEN DURING RESTORATION. ■■ CABINETS IN THE KITCHEN OF THE ROBINSON HOUSE, DURING RESTORATION. ■■ A ROLLING BAR FOR DISHTOWELS IN THE KITCHEN OF THE DEFOREST HOUSE. ■■ THE ANNUNCIATOR AT THE ROBINSON HOUSE SHOWED THE SERVANTS TO WHICH ROOM THEY WERE BEING CALLED. ■■ AN OUTSIDE SUPPLY-DELIVERY DOOR AT THE ROBINSON HOUSE ALSO RECEIVED THE SAME BOARD-AND-BATTEN TREATMENT AS THE INTERIOR.

THE KITCHEN OF THE 1906 DeFOREST HOUSE HAS REMAINED SURPRISINGLY INTACT. THE ORIGINAL PORCELAIN SINK IS SET OFF BY A SMALL WOODEN MOLDING OVER THE TOP AND SIDES. THE WOODEN DRAINBOARDS ARE STILL IN REMARKABLY GOOD CONDITION. THE BATTENS ON THE DOORS ARE ATTACHED BY THE ROUND-HEADED SCREWS FOR A DECORATIVE EFFECT. UNDER THE DRAINBOARDS, THE CABINET SIDES ARE JOINED WITH DOWELED JOINTS. THE DOOR TO THE RIGHT, WITH ITS ROLLING TOWEL BAR, LEADS TO A UTILITY AREA. TO THE RIGHT OF IT IS A GLIMPSE OF NEW CABINETS THAT WERE ADDED IN THE STYLE OF THE OLDER ONES.

A NEW KITCHEN IN THE CARRIAGE HOUSE OF THE ROBINSON HOUSE HAS CABINETS THAT MATCH THE ONES IN THE MAIN HOUSE. MODERN APPLIANCES, INCLUDING A DISHWASHER AND TWO UNDER-THE-COUNTER REFRIGERATORS, ARE HIDDEN BEHIND THE LARGE DOORS.

Although Katherine Duncan's original house was not designed by the Greenes, they designed additions and alterations in 1903 and for a subsequent owner, Theodore Irwin, in 1906 that are so well integrated it is hard to separate the elements of the original house. In the butler's pantry, tall fir cabinets have board-and-batten doors as well as a combination of brass cupboard turns and wooden knobs. Drawers have brass pulls. A nickel silver sink in a pine counter was provided for dishwashing. The oak floor is a more recent addition. These cabinets are more rustic than the Greenes' later work.

Nuts and Bolts

Many Hands Make Light Work

The majority of early-twentieth-century houses in urban and sub-urban areas had electricity, though not as much as we would consider adequate today. It was still a new technology and not altogether reliable, so some builders hedged by also putting in gas. Because it was new technology, most kitchens had at least one ceiling fixture, sometimes a wall light by the sink and maybe a light over the range. In the early part of the century, these tended to be of the bare-lightbulb-on-a-cord variety, though

A MOLDED ETCHED-GLASS SHADE DISTINGUISHES THE ORIGINAL HANGING FIXTURE IN THIS FORMER BREAKFAST ROOM. ONCE, A WALL WHERE THE DISHWASHER IS NOW HAD DIVIDED THIS KITCHEN INTO TWO TINY ROOMS.

later they evolved into simple pendant fixtures and sconces. Often the light was the only electrical source in the kitchen, and if you wanted to plug in something, it was necessary to unscrew the bulb and screw in a plug; fixtures tended to hang fairly low because of this. Many also lacked wall switches and had to be turned on with a keyed switch on the socket. At the time, it was felt that the bulbs also needed to be shaded (at least in the formal rooms) because they were so bright. In reality, the bulbs were the equivalent of, maybe, 40 watts. Electricity was introduced quite early in the century in some areas and quite late in others, but generally more lights and outlets could be found in the twenties and thirties, though certainly not enough to meet modern codes. Wiring was the knob-and-tube variety, and most bungalows had only 30-amp or possibly 60-amp service. There is nothing inherently wrong with this type of wiring, provided the insulation on the wires is still intact and no one has spliced into it in ways that are unsafe.

The bare-lightbulb-on-a-cord fixtures generally hung from a white porcelain ceiling canopy, although brass canopies were also found. The cord was either two twisted cloth-covered wires or the twisted wires were covered with a single cloth tube. Pendant fixtures and sconces were brass or nickel-plated brass, simple in design, with clear, frosted, or milk-glass shades. Pendants hung from chains or rods and were usually one- or two-arm fixtures. Multi-armed chandeliers were not found in kitchens, nor were art-glass shades. A breakfast room or nook might have had a pendant with an etched or hand-painted glass shade that was slightly fancier.

Many labor-saving electrical devices were invented early in the twentieth century, including toasters, waffle irons, electric mixers, irons, and, of course, electric refrigerators, which resulted in a few more electrical outlets being installed in the 1910s, 1920s, and

CLOCKWISE FROM TOP: THIS IS THE SAME FIXTURE SHOWN ON OPPOSITE PAGE WITH A DIFFERENT SHADE. A VARIETY OF SHADES ARE MADE THAT USE THE SAME SIZE FITTER (THE PIECE THAT HOLDS THE SHADE), ALLOWING FOR MANY DIFFERENT LOOKS USING THE SAME BASIC PARTS. ■■ FIXTURES WITH SCHOOLHOUSE SHADES ARE ONE OF THE MOST COMMON KITCHEN FIXTURES, EITHER CEILING-MOUNTED (LEFT) OR PENDANT STYLE (RIGHT). ■■ THE CLASSIC FIXTURE FOR KITCHENS, UTILITY ROOMS, BATHROOMS, HALLWAYS, AND ATTICS, THIS BULB HANGING FROM A MAROON CLOTH-COVERED CORD MAY BE A BIT TOO UTILITARIAN FOR MOST PEOPLE. A REPRODUCTION ANTIQUE BULB HELPS THE LOOK. ■■ A BRACKETED WALL FIXTURE LIKE THIS WAS OFTEN FOUND OVER THE SINK OR RANGE. IT COULD BE INSTALLED POINTING UP OR DOWN. ■■ VARIATIONS ON THIS SQUARE CANOPY WALL BRACKET ARE EXTREMELY COMMON IN ARTS & CRAFTS HOMES. THE SIMPLE DESIGN OF THIS FIXTURE WAS FOUND NOT ONLY IN THE KITCHEN, BUT IN THE LIVING ROOM, DINING ROOM, OR BEDROOMS AS WELL. (PHOTOS COURTESY REJUVENATION LAMP AND FIXTURE COMPANY)

The bare lightbulb hanging from a chain and a porcelain canopy has been dressed up with a ribbed-glass holophane shade in this butler's pantry.

Right: Somewhat fancier than a bare lightbulb on a cord, these nickel-plated pendant fixtures are still very simple and appropriately scaled for this large kitchen.

Obsessive Restoration

Existing period light fixtures can certainly be reused. If the wiring is frayed, they can be rewired. Ceiling fixtures often got painted right along with the ceiling, but paint can easily be stripped from metal parts with TSP or paint stripper. Many salvage yards and antiques dealers sell period fixtures, and many fine reproductions are available as well. Even the bare-lightbulb-on-a-cord variety is available as a reproduction, as are push-button light switches. Fixtures should be very simple.

Some areas of the country have energy-saving regulations that require a hard-wired fluorescent as the main light in the kitchen. A fluorescent is highly inappropriate in an old house. This is one place to make an exception to the "no art-glass fixtures in the kitchen" rule, since art glass does a fine job of softening the dreadful color of fluorescent lights.

Electrical outlets are a little harder to deal with. Leave the old wiring alone as long as it is in good condition. Any new wiring will most likely have to comply with current building codes, which means putting outlets every four feet and using the GFCI (Ground Fault Circuit Interrupter). It's hard to make a GFCI look old, but it's possible to get around the problem by installing a GFCI breaker at the panel for the whole circuit. The outlets, however, will still have to be grounded three-hole outlets, which will not look like the old two-hole outlets.

If the local building department allows, there are a couple of methods for disguising the outlets: put the outlets right up underneath the upper cabinets (this works especially well if new cabinets are being made—they can have a deep apron at the bottom to hide the outlets); or use plug-mold, a square wire conduit with an outlet every twelve inches, which can also be run up underneath the cabinets.

It is particularly difficult to add outlets to an existing tile backsplash, although it can be done. It is probably best left to a professional (if you can find someone with experience in that sort of thing) or considered as a

THIS IS A VERY TYPICAL CEILING-MOUNTED CANOPY THAT COULD BE USED WITH MANY DIFFERENT SHADES. SCHOOLHOUSE SHADES WERE COMMON, BUT GLOBES, OPEN SHADES, AND, IN LATER KITCHENS, MORE DECO-LOOKING SHADES WOULD ALSO HAVE BEEN USED. (PHOTO COURTESY REJUVENATION LAMP AND FIXTURE COMPANY)

last resort. If possible, try to figure out the location of studs, plumbing, and other obstructions before cutting holes in the tile for the electrical boxes—there will be no second chance. You might want to dummy-up some tile set in mortar to practice on first. Mask off the surrounding tile with sheet metal or quarter-inch metal flat bar held with double-sided carpet tape or duct tape to avoid damaging the surrounding tile, and be very careful when cutting. Use a diamond blade on a high-speed mini-grinder. Expect a lot of dust, sparks, and heat, so have an assistant with a shop vacuum and a spray bottle. The drill bit will become red-hot and break very quickly; cooling it with water from a spray bottle will prolong its life. The grinder won't cut all the way into the corners, but a small hammer drill with an eighth-inch bit works well for finishing up, or even a rotary (Dremel) tool will work (with a lot of patience). Make a dotted line of perforations in the corners—try not to drill all the way through the tile (put a cork over the drill bit so it stops at a certain depth). When the corners are perforated, you can break them out using a thin carbide-tipped chisel available from tile suppliers. An oversized outlet cover will disguise some of the damage if things don't go well.

Compromise Solution

There were no recessed downlights. Period. Don't have them. Don't let your architect, contractor, or lighting designer talk you into them. There was no under-cabinet lighting either. You may have as many visible sconces, pendants, and ceiling-mounted fixtures as you like. The trend at the moment seems to be more lighting than anyone really needs, which then has to be put on dimmer switches because that much light is too bright. Try to resist this trend and go with ceiling-mounted or pendant fixtures, or wall sconces.

Wiring to modern code will mean outlets every four feet or so, as well as GFCI outlets. Again, a GFCI circuit breaker can be used at the panel. Otherwise, it is possible to buy GFCI outlets with same-color TEST/RESET buttons rather than the red/black buttons used on most. For some reason, horizontal outlets are less visually obtrusive than vertically oriented plugs. The square "decor"-style outlets are too modern looking; try to stick with the standard outlets.

COPPER SINKS LIKE THIS ONE WERE COMMON IN BUTLER'S PANTRIES. THIS ONE SITS IN A MAHOGANY COUNTERTOP.

1930s. Push-button light switches were most common before the 1920s but were gradually replaced by brown Bakelite switches similar to the toggle switches in use today.

THAT SINKING FEELING

With the introduction of indoor plumbing, the "dry sinks" of the nineteenth century—wood-encased basins of cast iron, zinc, soapstone, or granite—gave way to all-metal or cast-iron sinks on legs with hot and cold taps. Early models were either plain and functional or quite elaborately decorated. In the early twentieth century, these were replaced by porcelain or porcelain-enameled cast-iron sinks with integral backsplash and drain board(s); the old-fashioned plain cast-iron, soapstone, and zinc-lined sinks had fallen into disfavor because of concerns about sanitation. Also, porcelain was more affordable at that point. Often the drain boards were made of wood with grooves to direct water back to the basin. Sinks stood on two or four legs or were hung on the wall. The space beneath the fixture was left open to allow for air circulation, as it was believed that moisture allowed germs and disease to breed.

In the 1910s, 1920s, and 1930s, these gradually gave

A SIMPLE CEILING-MOUNTED FIXTURE LIKE THIS IS A GOOD SUBSTITUTE FOR THE RECESSED DOWNLIGHTS ARCHITECTS OFTEN INSIST ON. (PHOTO COURTESY REJUVENATION LAMP AND FIXTURE COMPANY)

way to "tile-in" sinks set into tiled countertops, which often sloped toward the sink for drainage. These were usually set on cabinets, but the area directly under the sink remained open or was closed off with partial doors. Most sinks had one bowl, but two-bowl sinks were also available "for tidy maids who like to wash in soapy and rinse in clean hot water," according to *The Outlook* magazine in 1906. The magazine also mentions a rubber tube with spray attachment that could be screwed to the hot-water tap for rinsing. Some sinks had an electric dishwasher built into one bowl, or had one deep bowl for laundry, which was usually covered by a removable drain board. In the 1920s,

methods of producing colored porcelain were perfected, giving rise to colored sinks. In butler's pantries, sinks of copper or nickel silver (also called German silver, though it is not really silver at all but an alloy of copper, nickel, and zinc) were often installed, perhaps in the belief that metal sinks would be kinder to fine china and glassware.

One thing to keep in mind about sinks is that plumbing fixtures change very slowly. It was possible to buy a claw-foot bathtub from 1860 until well into the 1930s, and porcelain sinks on legs were still being offered until the start of World War II.

No discussion of sinks would be complete without a

CLOCKWISE FROM TOP: A VINTAGE DISHDRAINER FILLED WITH DEPRESSION GLASS SITS ON A TILE COUNTER FROM THE 1920S. LARGE-SIZED HEXAGONAL TILES WERE LESS COMMON THAN THE ONE-INCH SIZE, BUT THE COMBINATION OF BLACK AND WHITE WITH AN ACCENT COLOR IS TYPICAL. ▪▪ THE SINK IN THIS BUTLER'S PANTRY STILL HAS ITS ORIGINAL SLANTED WOODEN DRAINBOARDS. THE SEPARATE HOT AND COLD TAPS AND SUBWAY TILE BACKSPLASH WERE STANDARD IN 1910 WHEN THIS HOUSE WAS BUILT. ▪▪ EXPOSED PLUMBING GAVE WAY TO PARTIAL DOORS UNDER THE SINK, WHICH EVENTUALLY GAVE WAY TO VENTILATED DOORS WITH CANE INSERTS LIKE THESE. ▪▪ DETAIL OF A WOODEN DRAINBOARD AT THE DEFOREST HOUSE BY GREENE AND GREENE.

mention of dishwashing. Concerns about sanitation in the late nineteenth and early twentieth centuries gave rise to numerous articles and instructions about the proper way to wash dishes. Two pans (or a divided sink) for washing and rinsing were recommended. Tools included a dish mop, dishcloths, a bottle brush, a dish drainer (usually wire but occasionally wood), a soap shaker (a closed wire basket on a handle with a piece of soap in it—there were

no liquid detergents), a wire brush for pots, and tea towels for drying. Glasses and flatware were to be washed first, followed by plates and bowls, then the pots and pans. A multi-armed rack for drying the towels hung near the window, where it was thought that air circulation would dry them faster. In homes with a butler's pantry, a sink was often provided so that the fine china and glassware could be washed there and never enter the kitchen.

Obsessive Restoration

A porcelain sink with drain boards is worth keeping if it's in good condition. Small chips and nicks can be retouched with porcelain repair kits or appliance touch-up paint. So-called "reglazing," which is really just high-tech paint, is not recommended for kitchen sinks, as they are subject to hard wear and the paint really won't hold up. Another problem with old sinks is that the enamel has worn off in places, making them very porous and difficult to keep clean. It can help somewhat, once the sink is relatively clean, to use Gel-gloss or other fiberglass cleaner/sealers. They will make the surface a little less porous.

In the past as it is today, 99 percent of the sinks were white. If by some chance you are blessed with an intact colored sink, go to any lengths to keep it! They are quite rare, having evidently found less popularity in kitchens than in bathrooms. Obviously a sink on legs will be open underneath, as is proper. If this is bothersome, there is precedent for setting the sink on top of cabinets, although usually the plumbing would remain exposed.

A porcelain sink with drain boards from a salvage yard (if it's in good condition) will not be cheap but will be worth it for the look. In a later kitchen (from the late 1910s to the 1930s), a tile-in sink (usually one bowl) is appropriate. These were often quite shallow (5 to 6 inches deep), and usually the drain was near the side rather than in the middle as is common now. The drains tended to be small (1¼ to 1½ inches in diameter) with nonremovable strainers. Larger drains with removable strainers began to appear in the 1930s. (Actually, the drainpipe itself wasn't any larger, only the hole in the sink.) Tile-in sinks are still available new.

Sometimes a wall-hung sink was built into a run of cabinets. This one has wooden drainboards, now painted. One problem with many of these sinks is their shallowness, which makes draining pasta quite dangerous. This kitchen has yet to be restored and still wears its unfortunate self-adhesive vinyl wallcovering.

Compromise Solution

Personal preference will play a large role in choosing an appropriate sink. There are those who prefer one bowl and those who prefer two. Either porcelain on cast iron or all china is best. (Stainless steel, although first advertised in 1927, did not find widespread use in home kitchens until after World War II.) The currently popular farmhouse-style sinks are only appropriate for pre-1910 kitchens. Stone sinks of similar design in soapstone, granite, or slate, although not common, could also have been found in that period. Though many period sinks had rolled edges and possibly sat on cabinets, there was nothing used like the modern self-rimming sink that sits on the countertop, so that style should be avoided. Most kinds of undermount or tile-in sinks will work. Keep in mind that until the 1930s, most faucets were wall-mounted, not deck-mounted, so order the sink without holes. (As discussed under "Dishwashers," this makes it difficult to find a place for the air gap.) Modern-looking gadgets like soap dispensers, spray attachments, and instant hot-water dispensers should be avoided. Stick to white, since colored sinks now will not match the period colors. If you simply must have a hand-hammered copper sink, put it in the butler's pantry.

CROSS-HANDLED HOT AND COLD TAPS COMPLEMENT THIS COPPER SINK IN A BUTLER'S PANTRY.

TAP DANCING

Before indoor plumbing, many sinks contained a pump for drawing water from a well or cistern. When hot- and cold-running water came into the house, it was a great step forward. Early faucets had separate hot and cold taps and had a tendency to leak, though improvements in design eventually fixed that problem. A modern-style mixing faucet is mentioned in *The House Beautiful* as early as 1905 but evidently didn't catch on, as mixing faucets didn't become prevalent till the 1920s and 1930s. Most faucets were wall-mounted until the 1930s, when deck-mounted faucets began to make an appearance. Faucets were either plain brass or brass plated with nickel, until chromium plating began to replace nickel in the mid-1930s. Faucets mostly had lever or cross handles of either metal or porcelain, usually marked for "hot" and "cold." (It was new technology, not yet standardized, so explanation was needed.) Often a built-in soap dish was included.

Obsessive Restoration

Existing faucets may or may not be at the end of their useful life. Leakage can sometimes be repaired by rebuilding them with new washers and possibly grinding the valve seats a little. Sometimes they are beyond fixing; luckily, many fine reproduction faucets are available. Sometimes new handles are all that's required. Since valve stems are not standardized (each manufacturer is different), it's hard to find new handles to fit old valve stems. A salvage yard will be the best place to look. Be sure to take the valve stems with you for fitting. Old faucets can also be replated (if nickel). Reproduction faucets in a variety of styles and price ranges are available, including separate taps for the truly obsessive restorer. (Since mixing faucets were available in 1905, it might not be too much of a compromise to have one.)

A MODERN EUROPEAN FAUCET HAS AN OLD-FASHIONED FEEL, ALTHOUGH IT HAS A SINGLE-LEVER MECHANISM. NEXT TO IT, A SIMILAR-STYLED SOAP DISPENSER CONTAINS DISHWASHING LIQUID. THE ORIGINAL CABINETS OF THE KITCHEN AND ADJOINING BUTLER'S PANTRY (A WALL WAS REMOVED) HAVE UNFORTUNATELY LOST THEIR UPPER SLIDING DOORS BUT STILL RETAIN THEIR CHARM.

Compromise Solution

As mentioned at left, many fine reproduction faucets are available. There are even some single-lever models that look old, and wall-mounted faucets look more authentic. Historic brass faucets were not lacquered, so they tarnished. Think of it as patina, and avoid modern "permanently shiny" brass faucets. If tarnish bothers you, stick with nickel or chrome plating.

Nickel plating was probably the most common and is harder to find today. Chrome is an acceptable substitute, although nickel has a softer look. Cross or lever handles in metal or porcelain will look most appropriate. Bear in mind that faucets were utilitarian, so a really fancy faucet with hand-painted porcelain handles and a spout in the shape of a fish would not be right for a kitchen.

PLUMB THE DEPTHS

Indoor plumbing is probably the basis of modern civilization and certainly one of the most important factors in the development of the modern kitchen. By the twentieth century, water-supply pipes of galvanized iron or copper brought hot- and cold-running water into the kitchen. Hot water was provided by a water heater connected to the stove. Drains and traps were exposed because it was believed to be more "sanitary" and were either nickel-plated (later chrome-plated) or painted to match the wall. Supply lines were usually inside the wall but were sometimes exposed as well.

AIR APPARENT

In the late nineteenth and early twentieth centuries, there was much concern about what we would now call indoor air quality. Bad air was blamed for numerous diseases, and there was much advice about the proper way to ventilate the home. In the kitchen, the concern was to remove smoke, steam, and cooking odors. It was recommended that the kitchen have windows on at least two sides for cross-ventilation; however, builders often ignored this recommendation. There was a great deal of emphasis on the importance of the windows having intact screens to keep out insects.

In addition to windows, a hood over the stove was recommended, with a wide range of styles available. Some kitchens had large plaster or metal hoods that loomed over the stove, while others had only a modest cone- or pyramid-shaped indentation in the ceiling. The plaster hoods were quite thick (lath and plaster over 2 x 4s) and had rounded edges. Hoods used the chimney effect for passive ventilation: a hole at the top of the hood led to a duct that was vented through the roof. The larger hoods were occasionally tiled (inside or outside or both) and the metal or plaster was generally painted. Some kitchens had an electric ventilator, which was basically a large fan set into an outside wall or window.

IN MOST BUNGALOW KITCHENS, THE WATER WAS HEATED BY THE STOVE. THE HOT-WATER TANK WAS EITHER PART OF THE STOVE ITSELF OR A SEPARATE TANK SUCH AS THIS ONE (ALTHOUGH THIS ONE IS NOT HOOKED UP). ON THE WALL TO THE RIGHT OF THE TANK IS THE FLUE OPENING NEEDED FOR A GAS- OR WOODBURNING STOVE. SINCE THIS STOVE IS ELECTRIC, A METAL COVER REMINISCENT OF A PAPER PLATE HAS BEEN USED. EVEN TODAY, FLUE COVERS ARE STILL AVAILABLE AND ARE ALL PRINTED WITH COLORFUL SEASONAL VIEWS OF THE COUNTRYSIDE.

Scalloped partial doors hide the undersink plumbing in this 1922 kitchen. There seems to be endless variety in the patterns of these half-doors, which were most common in the 1920s and 1930s. Not pictured is a ventilation fan to the left of the sink.

PLUMBING

Obsessive Restoration

Modest houses generally had galvanized iron pipes. Galvanized pipes have gotten a bad reputation because after seventy or eighty years they tend to clog up with rust and deposits, which lower the water pressure, or rust out completely and begin to leak. Contractors will insist it all be ripped out and replaced with copper, but this will be expensive. Obviously, the parts that are completely rusted will have to go. However, if the only problem is deposit buildup, it tends to be worse in the hot-water pipes, especially the horizontal parts, so replacing only the hot-water side will often work wonders and save some money. Whether or not to replace with galvanized is a personal decision—it is still cheaper, but copper lasts a great deal longer. Nickel-plated drains and traps are still available

through various antique-plumbing-supply companies. Wall-mounted faucets don't have shut-off valves, which can be inconvenient, but these can be added with an access panel cut into the wall. If the water heater is still in the kitchen, unless it's an old instant heater that still functions, move it to the basement, utility porch, or a closet. Replacement with a modern instant heater (hidden somewhere) is another option.

Compromise Solution

There are those who find exposed plumbing unattractive. In that case, it would be best to hide it behind doors. Then whether to use copper, galvanized, or plastic supply lines and either plastic or chrome traps becomes mostly a matter of personal preference. Again, relocating the water heater is a good idea.

43

A RETRACTING HOOD SUCH AS THIS ONE MANUFACTURED BY BROAN HAS A SLIM PROFILE THAT FITS ALMOST FLUSH WITH THE CABINET. PULLING IT OUT ACTIVATES THE FAN AND A LIGHT.

VENTILATION

Obsessive Restoration

The main problem with existing hoods (particularly the large ones) is that they can overwhelm a kitchen, especially a small one, and the bottom edge is usually so low as to cause claustrophobia. It's a judgment call. A replacement hood could be made smaller and higher. The smaller indentation variety poses less of a problem. Either kind can be quite easily retrofitted with a fan for more efficient ventilation. A functioning through-the-wall fan should probably be kept.

Compromise Solution

A new stove hood can be fabricated in an old style, either of metal or plaster. Metal was painted, as a rule, although copper or brass hoods made an occasional appearance. These were not hammered—a hammered copper hood belongs on a fireplace. Stainless steel did not become common until after World War II. It's best to avoid really modern-looking hoods, although an exception can be made for "retractable" hoods available from a couple of manufacturers—these have a slim profile (the visible front piece is only 1¼ inches thick) and fit flush with the front of the upper cabinets above the stove. Of course, in a period kitchen there wouldn't be any cabinets above the stove.

Tʜɪs ᴏʀɪɢɪɴᴀʟ ɢʀᴇᴇɴ ʙᴀᴄᴋsᴘʟᴀsʜ ᴛɪʟᴇ ʀᴇᴍᴀɪɴᴇᴅ ᴡʜᴇɴ ᴛʜᴇ ʟᴏᴡᴇʀ ᴄᴀʙɪɴᴇᴛs ᴡᴇʀᴇ ʀᴇᴘʟᴀᴄᴇᴅ ɪɴ ᴛʜᴇ 1960s. Tʜᴇ ʟᴏᴜᴠᴇʀᴇᴅ ᴠᴇɴᴛ ᴏᴠᴇʀ ᴛʜᴇ Wᴇᴅɢᴇᴡᴏᴏᴅ sᴛᴏᴠᴇ ɪs ᴏᴘᴇʀᴀᴛᴇᴅ ʙʏ ᴄʜᴀɪɴs ʟᴀʙᴇʟᴇᴅ "ᴏᴘᴇɴ" ᴀɴᴅ "sʜᴜᴛ."

Rɪɢʜᴛ: A ᴛʜʀᴏᴜɢʜ-ᴛʜᴇ-ᴡᴀʟʟ ᴇxʜᴀᴜsᴛ ꜰᴀɴ ᴜsᴜᴀʟʟʏ ᴄᴀᴍᴇ ᴡɪᴛʜ ᴀ ᴄᴏᴠᴇʀ ᴛᴏ ᴘʀᴇᴠᴇɴᴛ ᴄᴏʟᴅ ᴀɪʀ ꜰʀᴏᴍ ᴄᴏᴍɪɴɢ ɪɴ ᴡʜᴇɴ ᴛʜᴇ ꜰᴀɴ ᴡᴀsɴ'ᴛ ɪɴ ᴜsᴇ. Tʜɪs ᴘᴀʀᴛɪᴄᴜʟᴀʀ ᴍᴏᴅᴇʟ ɪs ᴏᴘᴇʀᴀᴛᴇᴅ ʙʏ ᴀ ᴘᴜʟʟ-ᴄʜᴀɪɴ.

A MASSIVE CURVED PLASTER HOOD DOMINATES ONE SIDE OF THE KITCHEN IN THIS 1925 HOUSE, PROVIDING VENTILATION FOR THE REFURBISHED ELECTRIC STOVE. IN A SMALL KITCHEN, A HOOD THIS SIZE WOULD BE OVERWHELMING, BUT THIS KITCHEN IS LARGE ENOUGH FOR IT. TUCKED IN A NICHE IN THE CORNER IS A VINTAGE REFRIGERATOR WITH THE COMPRESSOR ON TOP (HIDDEN BY A HANGING BIRDCAGE). A PORCELAIN-TOPPED TABLE ON WHEELS PROVIDES A PORTABLE WORK SURFACE, AND BEHIND THE ARCH IS A SMALL BREAKFAST AREA.

LEFT: A PAINTED METAL HOOD DRAWS COOKING ODORS AND SMOKE OUT OF THIS 1931 KITCHEN. SINCE THIS HOOD IS A MODERN REPLACEMENT, IT CONTAINS A FAN AND A LIGHT, UNLIKE MOST OF THE OLDER HOODS THAT RELIED ON PASSIVE VENTILATION. THE STOVE IS ABOUT THE SAME AGE AS THE HOUSE.

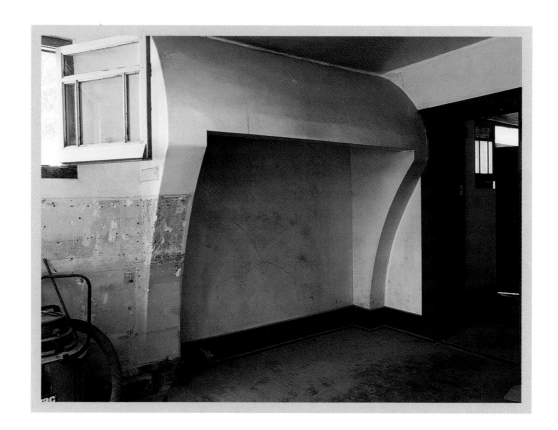

ALTHOUGH THERE IS NO STOVE UNDERNEATH AT THE MOMENT, THIS HOOD AT
THE ROBINSON HOUSE WAS OBVIOUSLY MADE FOR A RATHER LARGE
RANGE. THIS GREENE AND GREENE–DESIGNED HOUSE WAS IN THE MIDST OF
RESTORATION WHEN THIS PHOTO WAS TAKEN.

A THICK PLASTER HOOD DWARFS THIS 1930S STOVE AT THE GAMBLE HOUSE IN PASADENA, CALIFORNIA, DESIGNED BY GREENE AND GREENE. NOTE THE WOOD-WORK ON THE CEILING AROUND THE CHIMNEY, A DETAIL FEW OTHER ARCHITECTS WOULD HAVE BOTHERED WITH IN A KITCHEN. A DOOR TO THE LEFT OF THE STOVE LEADS TO THE COLD ROOM, WHERE THE ICEBOX AND OTHER STORAGE FOR PERISHABLE FOODS WAS LOCATED.

Eye Appeal

CALL ME A CABINET

From the turn of the century on, cabinets were fairly standardized, though variations in layout and combinations of doors, drawers, bins, and other storage options abounded. They were often built in place, so the back wall of the cabinet was the plastered kitchen wall; however, some were built in a cabinet shop and were likely backed with bead board (1 x 4-inch tongue-and-groove paneling, usually with a V-groove in the center). Upper cabinets were usually 12 inches deep and generally

SOME OF THE OWNERS' COLLECTION OF VINTAGE KITCHENWARE IS DISPLAYED HERE IN THE BUTLER'S PANTRY, INCLUDING A WARING BLENDER AND A DRINK MIXER. A PERIOD KITCHEN IS AN EXCELLENT OPPORTUNITY TO SHOWCASE THIS KIND OF COLLECTION. BELOW THIS CABINET, A STAIRWAY LEADS TO THE BASEMENT.

went all the way to the ceiling. A simple crown or cove molding finished them off at the top. They were hung lower than upper cabinets are today, usually about 12 inches above the counter, and sometimes sat on simple brackets. Some came all the way down to the countertop for a hutch effect. Sometimes there were two sets of doors, small ones across the top and longer ones below. Sliding doors on tracks were often used, though typically doors were hinged. Glass doors were commonly used in cabinets for storing dishes. The doors were either plain or muntin-patterned, often similar to the pattern of other built-ins in the house or echoing the muntin pattern of the windows, although oftentimes much simpler than what might be found in the dining or living room. In some houses, the dining-room china cabinet also had doors on the kitchen side, either glass or wood, so the clean dishes could be put back easily. Shelves inside could be fixed or adjustable. Open shelving, a hallmark of Victorian kitchens, was also quite common, especially before 1920.

Lower cabinets were usually about the same height as today (36 inches finished) but not as deep, anywhere from 15 to 22 inches. They sat directly on the floor and did not have toe-kicks like modern cabinets, except for under the sink, which was often left open or had partial doors. Infinite combinations of doors, drawers, tilt-out bins, and clever storage ideas abounded: things like fold-out tables, pull-out cutting boards and breadboards, metal-lined bins for flour and staples, small bins under the sink for storing soap and dish-washing items, fold-down shelves, even corner-cabinet lazy Susans similar to the ones found today. Drawers ran on simple wooden runners.

These glass-doored cabinets are topped with a wide rail and crown molding, which continues around the room as a decorative detail. They sit on simple brackets that extend to the countertop and have bead-board backs. The four small drawers below are just one of many variations found in old cabinets.

Cabinets were always face-framed, and doors were almost always inset (set into and flush with the face-frame when closed), although in the 1920s, overlay doors (sitting on top of the face-frame) like those found on Hoosier cabinets began to make an appearance. A 1928 article in *The Architect and Engineer* discussed "neatly designed and moulded panel doors with carefully rounded lips on the front [that] add to the beauty and avoid the unsightly crack as in the old-fashioned cupboard door." Doors were a frame-and-panel construction of square-cut stiles and rails around a flat panel (in modern parlance, usually called Shaker doors), although occasionally a small molding outlined the panel (more common in late Victorian and Edwardian cabinets). The stiles and rails were a full 1 inch thick.

In the western United States, cabinets were invariably made of vertical-grain Douglas fir (the inexpensive wood of its time—now more expensive than oak). In other locales, other softwoods were employed. Kitchen cabinets were rarely made of the sort of hardwoods that might be found

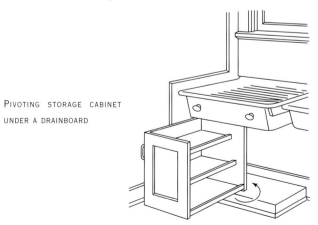

Pivoting storage cabinet under a drainboard

in the more formal rooms of the house. Cabinets were either varnished or painted with enamel.

One specialty cabinet found in many kitchens was the cooler cabinet. Rising from floor to ceiling, generally at one end of a run of cabinets and usually (though not always) on an outside wall, it was cooled by a draft effect: 1-inch-diameter holes drilled in the floor allowed cooler air to be drawn up from the basement or crawl space, and a vent at the top (either in the outside wall or into the attic) allowed warmer air to escape, setting up the chimney effect. Sometimes both vents were in the outside wall, and occasionally the whole thing was contained in an upper cabinet. Inside the cabinet, slatted or wire-mesh shelves allowed air to circulate. Sometimes the lower part of the cabinet contained deep drawers with wire-mesh bottoms, or occasionally the bottom part contained a small icebox. In cold climates, wooden covers could be used over the vents in winter. (In our energy-conscious times, many of these cabinets have been removed or had their vents covered with plywood or drywall—look for evidence of the vents on the outside wall of the house, or look for a pattern

NEW CABINETS WITH SHAKER-STYLE DOORS AND INSET DRAWERS HAVE CRAFTSMAN-INSPIRED DETAILS SEEN IN THE SMALL BRACKETS UNDER THE MOLDING AND COUNTERTOP, AS WELL AS THE LARGER BRACKETS UNDER THE UPPER CABINETS. MODERN CABINET OPTIONS, SUCH AS A PULL-OUT PANTRY (TO THE LEFT OF THE STOVE), A LAZY SUSAN (IN THE CORNER), AND A TILT-OUT TRAY (UNDER THE SINK), ARE HIDING BEHIND THE PERIOD-LOOKING DOORS.

of holes in the floor.) These cabinets are still a fine place to store potatoes, onions, garlic, wine, and such. The vent openings should be screened to keep out animals, and the doors can be weather-stripped and even insulated.

One period magazine also describes a similar type of cabinet used for storing dirty dishes out of sight until they could be washed: it was vented like a cooler cabinet, had slotted or wire shelves, and had doors on both the dining-room side and the kitchen side so the dirty dishes could be put in on one side and taken out on the other.

Another common specialty cabinet was the built-in ironing board. Most of them appear to have been designed for ironing while sitting down. If this feature is not appealing, the area can be turned into a spice cabinet. The water heater was sometimes placed in a cabinet or closet of its own, next to the stove.

Tilt-out bins (ill.) for flour and other staples were common. Although most of us no longer buy fifty pound bags of flour, bins can still be useful for storing bags of dog or cat food, recyclables, or even trash.

The most well-known specialty cabinet is the "Hoosier cabinet," named after the Hoosier Manufacturing Company of New Castle, Indiana. The Swiss Army Knife of cabinets, this multipurpose work center contained flour and sugar bins with sifters, a pull-out metal work surface, a spice rack, canisters, a cutting board, storage cupboards, drawers, and racks. Deluxe models boasted clocks, mirrors, ironing boards, and anything else the manufacturers could add on. Originally available in oak or white enamel, colored finishes also became available in the 1920s.

Island cabinets as we know them today were extremely rare, though many kitchens had worktables of one sort or another. Many

TOP: THESE FLOUR BINS HAVE WOODEN TOPS, PERHAPS TO DISCOURAGE VERMIN. THEY ARE PART OF A "COLD ROOM," A SCREENED PANTRY THAT ALSO CONTAINED THE ICEBOX. ■■ BOTTOM LEFT: A CLOSE-UP OF THE IRON STORAGE COMPARTMENT SHOWS THE IRON REST. LIGHTNING BOLTS ON THE DOOR SYMBOLIZED ELECTRICITY. ■■ RIGHT: THE DOOR ON THIS COOLER CABINET IS INSULATED AND FACED WITH BEAD BOARD.

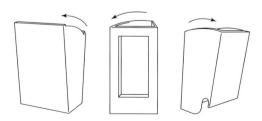

VARIOUS DESIGNS FOR FLOUR BINS. THE CENTER DESIGN PIVOTS OUT OF A CORNER CABINET.

were just tables, but others had drawers and doors and various kinds of built-in storage. Older versions, often called "baker's tables," were precursors of the Hoosier cabinet.

Clever built-ins can solve modern storage problems as well: a microwave oven can hide in a small cabinet with a drop-down front; an appliance garage with a real cabinet door instead of a tambour door would not look out of place on a counter; even the telephone can be hidden in a wall-hung cabinet. There is also precedent for the modern tilt-out tray for sponges in front of the sink.

New period-style cabinets will obviously need to be custom made, whether for obsessive restoration or compromise. Most stock cabinets, even those with Shaker-style doors, will invariably be of the invisible European-hinge, melamine-interior variety. The importance of the visual composition of face frames, doors, and hardware cannot be overemphasized.

Obsessive Restoration

Although plywood had been invented, cabinet sides, door panels, and drawer bottoms were made of edge-glued boards. Shop-built cabinets had backs of 1 x 4-inch tongue-and-groove beaded paneling. Although any kitchen magazine will tell you that dovetail joints are the mark of a well-crafted drawer, all the original drawers I have ever seen have half-lap or butt joints held together with glue and nails. The drawer face forms the fourth side of the drawer box on old drawers, unlike modern construction where the face is applied to an already completed box. Sometimes the drawer has a U-shaped

HERE IS A SET OF FLOUR BINS IN THE PASTRY KITCHEN AT THE 1899 DUNSMUIR HOUSE IN OAKLAND, CALIFORNIA. THE MARBLE SLAB ABOVE WAS USED FOR PREPARING DOUGH. ON THE FLOOR IS MARBLEIZED LINOLEUM IN A CHECKERBOARD PATTERN. CHECKED PATTERNS HAVE BEEN POPULAR IN SHEET FLOORING SINCE ITS INVENTION.

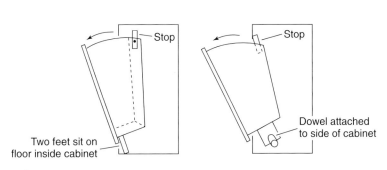

TILT-OUT BINS ARE CONSTRUCTED WITH A PIVOTING STOP THAT ALLOWS THE BIN TO BE REMOVED FOR CLEANING.

wooden runner on the bottom, which slides along a piece of wood inside the cabinet frame; otherwise the sides of the drawer slide along a frame inside the cabinet. Door frames and face frames were constructed using blind mortise-and-tenon joinery. If you want your new doors to be as thick as the old doors, construct them using 5/4 stock. (A 1 x 4 isn't as thick as it used to be.) The glass in glass doors is held in place by small square or quarter-round moldings attached with brads. The truly obsessive will want to use Restoration Glass from Bendheim or wavy glass salvaged from old windows.

Shelves could be either fixed or adjustable. Fixed shelves sat on cleats nailed to the sides of the cabinet. Adjustable shelves sat on cleats that fitted into slots cut into ½ x 1-inch strips of wood nailed to the sides of the cabinet. The ends of the shelves were notched to fit around the strips. There is even precedent for metal shelf pins that fit into drilled holes, similar to what is available now. Magazines at the time encouraged decorating shelf edges in glass door cabinets for a more attractive look as well as aesthetically arranging the dishes inside. Lace edging or decoratively cut and punched paper strips were considered appropriate. Shelf paper was recommended, and it may still be possible to buy actual paper shelf lining at your local hardware store. It was usually held in place with thumbtacks. Self-adhesive shelf covering was first manufactured in 1949. Scraps of leftover linoleum were also used as shelf lining.

As mentioned before, islands were rare and worktables were common, though some worktables very much resembled islands. Baker's tables and Hoosier cabinets were also common and are still available.

Many cabinets were painted with oil-based enamel in colors like cream, ivory, buff, or beige. Although period writings talk about white, pigments available at that time were not as bright as

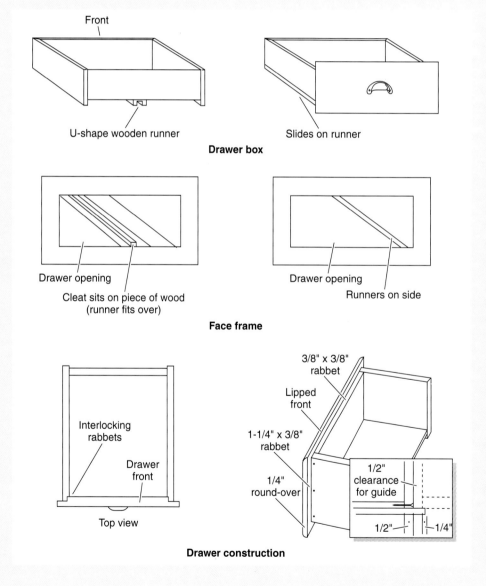

Front

U-shape wooden runner

Drawer box

Slides on runner

Drawer opening

Cleat sits on piece of wood
(runner fits over)

Face frame

Drawer opening

Runners on side

Interlocking
rabbets

Drawer
front

Top view

Drawer construction

3/8" x 3/8"
rabbet

Lipped
front

1-1/4" x 3/8"
rabbet

1/4"
round-over

1/2"
clearance
for guide

1/2"   1/4"

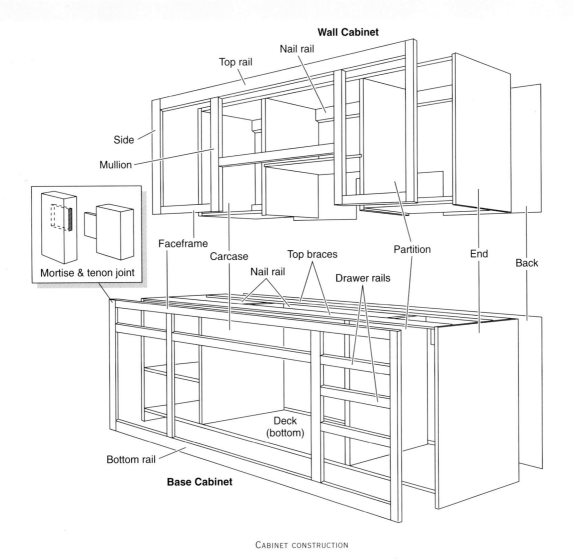

Wall Cabinet

Nail rail

Top rail

Side

Mullion

Facefame

Carcase

Top braces

Nail rail

Partition

End

Back

Drawer rails

Mortise & tenon joint

Deck (bottom)

Bottom rail

Base Cabinet

CABINET CONSTRUCTION

modern titanium-based white paints, so stick to off-white. In the twenties, more color (mostly pastel) made an appearance. Many cabinets that were originally varnished were painted later (strip off some paint with a heat gun and see if there's a layer of varnish underneath). Unpainted cabinets were usually finished with orange shellac. It gives a lovely dipped-in-honey appearance but has a tendency to darken and crack after seventy or eighty years. (It strips off easily with denatured alcohol.) As a finish, varnish can be damaged by water or alcohol, so it may not be the most practical thing to use.

On the other hand, it is easily renewed. Using varnish for the final coat is a good compromise. (See Bruce Johnson's *The Weekend Refinisher* for more information on finishes.)

Sometimes the original cabinets got a face-lift in the 1950s or 1960s and acquired new slab doors. These can be replaced with proper frame-and-panel doors; however, overlay rather than inset doors will fit better in this case, as the old openings will not be square and inset doors have fairly close tolerances.

LEFT: NEW DOORS, HARDWARE, TILE, AND A COAT OF PAINT TRANSFORMED THESE 1960S PLY-WOOD CABINETS INTO PERIOD-STYLE CABINETS. IT IS DIFFICULT TO FIT INSET DOORS INTO THE OUT-OF-SQUARE OPENINGS OF EXISTING CABINETS, SO OVERLAY DOORS ARE RECOMMENDED AND WOULD STILL BE APPROPRIATE TO THIS 1920S KITCHEN. ■■ RIGHT: THIS SMALL TILED ISLAND CONTAINS STORAGE FOR WINE AND OTHER ITEMS, AS WELL AS A POT RACK ABOVE. THE SHELVES BEHIND THE GLASS DOORS HAVE BEEN DECORATED WITH LACE-EDGED NAPKINS.

Compromise Solution

Plywood will make perfectly acceptable sides, backs, drawer bottoms, and door panels. Avoid MDF (medium-density fiberboard) and particle board—they do not hold up well. Have cabinets with a toe-kick if you like. Plywood paneling that resembles bead board is available for visible cabinet backs. There is no substitute for frame-and-panel doors, but biscuit or other types of joinery would work as well as mortise-and-tenon. Doors made with 1 x 4 stock will not be as thick as old doors, but few people will notice. Glass can be mounted using silicone adhesive instead of molding. Drawer boxes can be made in the modern manner and run on metal glides. Center-mount glides that don't show when the drawer is open are also available.

As noted before, there were few islands in the sense we think of them now, but some worktables greatly resembled islands. They did not, however, have sinks or cooktops in them. An island is a pretty good place to hide a dishwasher, though, if the original cabinets are not deep enough to accommodate one.

Modern shelf-mounting systems are acceptable, either shelf pins in drilled holes or clips that fit into metal tracks. In a glass-doored cabinet, the drilled-hole method might be visually less obtrusive. Self-adhesive shelf covering is acceptable.

Oil-based enamel is still available, but latex semi-gloss is a perfectly fine substitute. In clear finishes, varnish or lacquer is fine. Polyurethane has too much of a plastic look. Avoid modern finishes like thermofoil.

B RASS BIN HANDLES AND CUPBOARD TURNS WERE THE MOST COMMON TYPES OF HARDWARE FOR CABINETS. USUALLY MADE OF STAMPED RATHER THAN CAST METAL, THEY WERE GENERALLY PLATED. THE PINK COLOR OF THIS BUTLER'S PANTRY, ALTHOUGH IT ACTUALLY DATES FROM THE 1950S, WAS ALSO POPULAR IN THE 1920S.

HANDLE(S) WITH CARE

Period cabinet hardware was remarkably standardized. There are about twelve different types of hinges, pulls, and knobs, with a few style variations in each category. Window hardware styles were equally limited. Cabinet doors were hinged with either 2½-inch ball-tipped mortise hinges or surface-mounted butterfly hinges. Overlay doors, such as those found on Hoosier cabinets, used special surface-mounted overlay hinges. Butterfly hinges came in about four basic shapes.

The most common door hardware was the spring-loaded cupboard turn, followed by hexagonal glass knobs in clear, white, or colored glass; white porcelain knobs; and round or square wooden knobs. Doors closed with ball catches set into the edge of the door. In the 1930s, some metal knobs started to appear. Hoosier cabinets had special offset latches for the doors.

Drawers opened using bin pulls (the most common), glass "bridge" handles (clear, white, or colored), or metal drawer pulls. Metal hardware was either brass- or nickel-plated (chrome plating began to appear in the 1930s). Most of it was not solid brass but plating over base metal, and most pieces were stamped rather than cast.

Double-hung windows used the still-ubiquitous sash lock and lifts; casement windows used hardware similar to modern hardware, although many houses had a looped-style turn that is harder to find now. Casement operators for kitchen windows usually consisted of a hook-and-eye system, where the hook part was 8 to 12 inches long and screwed into the sill, and eyes located in various places on the sash regulated how far the window opened. Operable transom windows used special catches similar to cupboard catches.

These custom cabinets have invisible European hinges, though the doors are inset. Original cabinets always have visible hinges since European hinges are a fairly recent invention. The difference is quite subtle and unlikely to be noticed by most people.

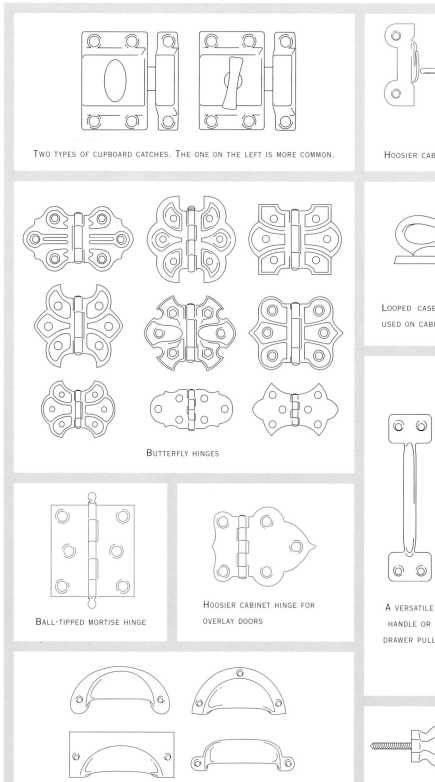

Two types of cupboard catches. The one on the left is more common.

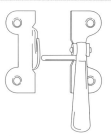

Hoosier cabinet latch

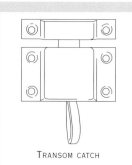

Transom catch

Butterfly hinges

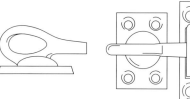

Looped casement fastener. These were occasionally used on cabinets.

Ball-tipped mortise hinge

Hoosier cabinet hinge for overlay doors

A versatile handle or drawer pull

Casement operator

Bin pulls

Hexagonal glass knob and bridge handle

FROM LEFT: HEAVY NICKEL-PLATED HARDWARE ADORNS THIS TINY ICEBOX. ▪▪ LOOPED CASEMENT HARDWARE USUALLY SEEN ON WINDOWS SECURES THESE CABINETS AT THE ROBINSON HOUSE BY GREENE AND GREENE. ▪▪ A VINTAGE ELECTRIC WALL HEATER WARMS THE KITCHEN AREA OF THE ROBINSON HOUSE. FEW OTHER ARCHITECTS WOULD HAVE CONSIDERED THE COMFORT OF SERVANTS.

Obsessive Restoration

If there is existing hardware in the kitchen, it is often covered with paint. If you can manage to get the hardware off, soak it in a strong mixture of hot TSP (about one tablespoon per cup of water) to take the paint off; more layers of paint will require more soaking. Paint stripper works also. The hardware may or may not be in good shape once it is stripped—it might be easier to buy new hardware, since most of the old styles are still being made. Cupboard turns of stamped and plated metal, various styles of butterfly hinges, brass drawer pulls, and wooden and porcelain knobs can still be purchased at hardware stores (metal hardware comes in brass or chrome only). Ball-tipped mortise hinges, Hoosier cabinet hinges and latches, hexagonal glass knobs, glass bridge handles and bin pulls, or any nickel-plated pieces are available through catalogs and specialty retailers. Casement latches with a looped-style turn, which were extremely common in the period, are quite difficult to find now. Salvage yards are the best source.

One final obsessive note: Use only slotted screws!

Although Phillips screws had been invented, they were not used residentially.

Compromise Solution

Hardware is like jewelry for the kitchen: the interplay of doors, drawers, hinges, and knobs is an important part of the design. Hinges were meant to be visible, and there were no hidden self-adjusting European hinges in the period. Though cabinetmakers like European hinges because they are easier to install, cabinets without visible hinges just don't look right. Surface-mounted hinges are easier to work with than mortise hinges (which may be enough to placate the cabinetmaker). Since appropriate period hardware is available, there is no need to compromise on that. Price might come into the picture: solid brass cupboard turns cost about eight times as much as stamped ones, glass bridge handles are expensive, and nickel plating costs more than brass. If there are a lot of cabinets, it can add up. On the other hand, very few people will notice whether the screws are slotted or have a Phillips head.

COUNTER ESPIONAGE

WOOD

FROM TOP: THESE 2-INCH HEX TILES HAVE ACCENTS THAT MATCH THE EDGE TILE AND LINER STRIP. ■■ CLOSE-UP OF COUNTER SHOWING THE RUNNING BOND PATTERN OF THE MOSAIC. ■■ CLOSE UP, THE KNOT-WORK PATTERN OF THIS MOSAIC COUNTERTOP IS REVEALED, ALONG WITH SOME MONITOR-TOP SALT AND PEPPER SHAKERS.

Wood was by far the most prevalent countertop material, either as a finished top or a base for other materials, and it is still used that way today. Douglas fir, pine, oak, maple, and mahogany were commonly used. Hardwoods like cherry or exotic woods like teak were not unheard of. Bead-board wainscoting often continued around the room behind the cabinets and served as a backsplash. Wooden drain boards near the sink were common in late-nineteenth- and early-twentieth-century kitchens, later giving way to porcelain sinks with built-in drain boards and, eventually, porcelain sinks surrounded by tile. Even with tile around the sink area, the remaining countertops were often made of wood.

LINOLEUM

Eventually it occurred to someone that since linoleum held up so well on the floor, it would also be good on the counter. Probably it was added to a lot of previously wooden counters but was still being used well into the 1930s and 1940s, usually with the metal edge banding associated with laminate counters from that period. It does make an excellent countertop, although it is prone to water damage if used around a sink.

CERAMIC TILE

Tile found its way onto walls and floors before it made an appearance on countertops. It began to appear even before 1900 and was common by the teens, most often plain white tiles on counter and backsplash around a tile-in sink. The tiled countertop slanted toward the sink for drainage, and, occasionally, colored-edge tiles or narrow stripes of color in the backsplash appeared.

The 1920s and 1930s were the real heyday of tile. White tile continued to be quite popular, usually oblong tiles (3 x 6 inches) laid in running bond on the backsplash, and either 1-inch hexagonal mosaics or square (3 x 3 inches, 4¼ x 4¼ inches) tiles on the counter with quarter-round tiles bordering the sink and finishing off the backsplash. Box-cap tiles finished the front edges of the counter, often in contrasting colors. Colored tile became popular during this period:

A BLUE LINOLEUM COUNTER, WHICH MATCHES THE FLOOR, TOPS THESE METAL CABINETS, A LATER ADDITION TO THIS KITCHEN AT THE BENNETT RANCH IN LAKE FOREST, CALIFORNIA. LINOLEUM MAKES A HIGHLY PRACTICAL COUNTERTOP IN AREAS THAT ARE NOT SUBJECT TO WATER OR HEAT.

pastels such as yellow, green, blue, peach, beige, or pink were often combined with darker edging tiles in black, burgundy, green, blue, or red. A narrow (½ x 6 inches) multicolored "feature strip" was incorporated into the backsplash, and colored accent tiles also decorated the countertop. None of this was "art tile" in the Arts & Crafts sense. Art tile was limited to the more formal rooms of the house as fireplace surrounds, flooring, and such. Possibly the owner of a tile company or someone very wealthy might have art tile in the kitchen as a way of showing off, but it was extremely rare.

Tile was laid on a reinforced mortar bed approximately 1 inch thick. Grout joints were minimal, less than $\frac{1}{16}$ inch. Mosaics came in sheets with a paper backing on the face of the tile. After the tile was set, the paper was sponged with water till the glue dissolved and the paper could be peeled

off. Sometimes, 3- and 4-inch-square tiles were laid on the diagonal with a square border around the edge. Small (1 x 2 inches) rectangular tiles in a herringbone pattern were less common but not unknown, as was oblong tile or 1-inch-square mosaic tile laid in a running-bond pattern. White 1-inch hexagonal tiles were probably the most common.

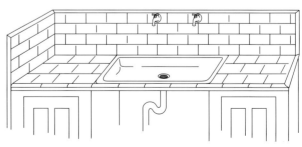

TILED DRAINBOARD

STONE

Stone countertops of marble, granite, slate, or soapstone were occasionally found, mostly in areas where that type of stone was quarried locally and in the kitchen of the quarry's owner(s). A marble pastry slab might have been found in the kitchens of the wealthy or upper middle class, but for the most part, stone countertops were fairly rare. Lovely as it is, iridescent rainbow granite has no place in a period kitchen.

METAL

Zinc, tin, or copper countertops (often in conjunction with metal-lined dry sinks) were more common from the 1890s to the early 1910s. Pull-out metal work surfaces of aluminum or porcelain enamel were a feature of most Hoosier cabinets. Sinks and countertops of Monel metal (an alloy of nickel and copper) were occasionally found, especially in the 1920s. Enameled metal counters, while not common, did exist. Enamel-top tables were a very popular item.

A NEW MARBLE COUNTERTOP WAS INSTALLED IN THE SINK AREA OF THIS BUNGALOW, THOUGH THE OTHER COUNTERTOPS ARE WOOD (SEEN ON THE RIGHT). MARBLE NEEDS TO BE SEALED WITH MINERAL OIL OR STONE SEALER, AND IS SUSCEPTIBLE TO ACIDS. THE OWNER'S CAT AGREED TO POSE FOR THE PHOTO.

This cabinet retains the original wooden countertop. Most counters were made of a single piece of wood. Today it would be difficult to find a 1 x 20, but individual boards can be glued up to obtain the necessary width. These cabinet doors have a more interesting pattern than most.

Obsessive Restoration

Wooden countertops were often made of one piece of wood (1 or 2 inches thick by up to 24 inches wide). At the present time it is difficult, though not impossible, to get a piece of wood this size. A plank that wide is more likely to cup or crack; so, many times, smaller edge-glued boards were used instead. Wooden drain boards should either be made of rot-resistant wood like teak, redwood, or cypress, or they will need several coats of spar varnish, which will need to be touched up frequently. Drain boards should be slanted toward the sink, and grooves can be routed into them, if desired. Other wooden countertops should also be varnished or oiled or they will stain easily.

Linoleum countertops need either a metal or wooden edge to finish them off, and the linoleum should be waxed periodically with floor wax or paste wax.

Tile was always laid on a mortar bed, which consisted of the following layers: rough wood planks covered with a layer of building felt (tar paper), then wire-mesh reinforcing (chicken wire) held by bent-over nails, followed by a layer of mortar about an inch thick, into which the tile was laid. Tiles were spaced very closely so grout joints were minimal or nonexistent. Box-cap edging is no longer made, but box edging is still available from some small manufacturers. There are a couple of ways to use it: cut off one leg of the U and run it vertically or use it horizontally on top of the counter, with one leg hanging off the edge and sitting on either a strip of wood or a row of 3 x 6-inch surface bull-nose-edge tiles. The other problem with modern box edge is the lack of accompanying trim pieces such as outside corners and end pieces, resulting in corners having to be mitered. Also available was ogee edging (S-shaped), similar to modern V-cap edging but with a more rounded profile. Modern V-cap came into production after Word War II.

Old tile is sharp-edged, unlike modern tile with eased edges. (Some flat tile is still made, but it is difficult to find.) Machine-made tile with eased edges began to appear with the advent of thin-set mortar after World War II; cutting the tile by machine tended to compress the edges, and it was more difficult to make tile lay perfectly flat in the thin-set mortar. The sharp-edged tile made that more obvious, whereas eased edges disguised the imperfections in laying. Modern tile also tends to come with spacing lugs on the sides, resulting in wider grout joints. These can be cut off with a wet saw to allow for narrower joints. One-inch hexagonal tile is

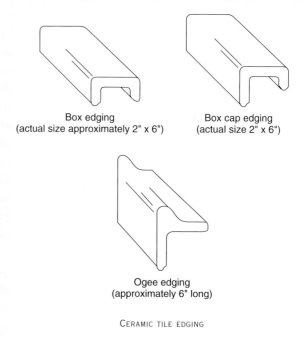

Box edging
(actual size approximately 2" x 6")

Box cap edging
(actual size 2" x 6")

Ogee edging
(approximately 6" long)

CERAMIC TILE EDGING

still widely available (the porcelain or vitreous tile holds up better on a counter). Tiles that are 4¼ x 4¼-inch square are widely available; 3 x 3-inch tiles are much harder to find; 3 x 6 inch oblong ("subway") tiles are still produced. Old-style mosaics (often a combination of 1- and 2-inch squares with 1 x 2-inch oblongs) are hard to find. Of course, salvaged tiles are possible, though acquiring sufficient quantities can be a problem. Damaged tiles (small gouges or cracks) can be filled with white thin-set mortar with the occasional use of porcelain touch-up paint; for colored tiles, try matching the color in nail polish.

Compromise Solution

Hardwood plywood with a wood strip or molding on the front edge is a reasonable substitute for solid wood. Butcher block is also acceptable.

Much period-looking tile is still available. Modern white glazes tend to be much whiter than their period counterparts, so look for antique white, cream, or almond. In colored tiles, similar colors to those used in the 1920s and 1930s are also available. Mosaic tiles are still available (1-inch hex, 1-inch squares, 2-inch squares), but they usually come in sheets spaced for ⅛-inch grout joints. If you want smaller joints, the sheets have to be cut up and the tiles placed individually. Modern V-cap is fine for edging. Try to avoid tiles larger than 4¼ x 4¼ inches; 6-inch, 8-inch, or 12-inch squares look too modern. Keep it simple. Fancy rope inlays and edging that resembles crown molding are not appropriate. And if you've just got to have art tile in your kitchen, frame some and hang it on the wall.

Setting the tile on cement board with thin-set mortar is an acceptable method. Don't go crazy with colored grout; white, off-white, sand, and gray were pretty much the period colors.

If you must have stone, you might want to limit it to just a few areas, perhaps around the sink and stove. And make it real stone, not that dreadful solid surfacing—it looks utterly fake. If you are on a very small budget, some of the matte-surface laminates, especially the vaguely stone-like ones, don't look too bad if you use a wood-edge treatment. Try to avoid the ubiquitous post-formed laminate countertops.

Also, there are a couple of companies that make porcelain-enamel countertops and tabletops on a custom basis.

FLOOR SHOW

The most common kitchen flooring was soft-wood, usually pine or fir, that was either painted or varnished. Hardwood was recommended by many experts at the time, but due to the expense, most builders stuck with soft-wood. Often the tongue-and-groove softwood was nailed directly to the floor joists, serving as both subfloor and finish floor. Period magazines mention that the junction of the wall with a wooden floor should be covered with quarter-round molding to prevent the accumulation of dirt. Ceramic tile was also recommended for its sanitary qualities, but actual tile installations were rare except in wealthy homes or the home of the tile-company owner.

Wood was soon superseded by linoleum, which remained the most popular kitchen flooring well into the 1950s. In fact, linoleum pretty much became the generic name for sheet flooring. Invented by Englishman Frederick Walton in 1863—and composed of ground cork, linseed oil, and fillers on a burlap backing—it became available in America in the 1870s.

Linoleum was either installed wall-to-wall or linoleum "rugs" were used over wood floors. Solid color "battleship" linoleum in colors such as dark gray, green, or brown and blue-and-white or black-and-white checkerboards were popular. Small tile-like patterns abounded. One of the most common, a random-sized square-and-rectangular-tile pattern (originally designated Armstrong 5352) is still produced in vinyl. In the 1920s and 1930s, an explosion of color and pattern took place: Florentine swirls, stylized Art Deco patterns, and even Oriental rug designs were produced. Many old linoleum patterns are still available in vinyl, although the really unusual ones are not. A well-cared-for linoleum floor can easily last thirty or forty years. Sometimes linoleum was given a coat of varnish, but usually it was just waxed.

Nineteenth-century linoleum had designs printed on the surface of a solid-color body; but then Walton discovered ways to integrate the designs into the body during the manufacturing process by mixing the linoleum granules in various ways before they were run through the heated rollers (called calenders) that fused them to the backing, resulting in marble, granite, and jaspé (striated) patterns.

FROM TOP: A PATTERN OF RANDOM SHAPES INTERSPERSED WITH FLOWERS IS NOT GENERALLY FOUND IN KITCHEN FLOORING, BUT THIS KITCHEN IS THE EXCEPTION. UNFORTUNATELY THE BITUMEN-IMPREGNATED FELT DOES NOT HOLD UP AS WELL AS REAL LINOLEUM, SO LARGE PARTS OF THIS FLOOR HAVE WORN THROUGH TO THE FELT. ■■ ANOTHER ORIENTAL RUG, THIS ONE MADE OF BITUMEN-IMPREGNATED FELT, DECORATES THE ATTIC IN THIS BUNGALOW. MOST OF THE BEDROOMS ALSO HAVE RUGS OF THIS TYPE. ■■ THIS LINOLEUM WAS INLAID AT THE FACTORY AND IS ORIGINAL TO THIS DEPRESSION-ERA HOUSE, WHERE IT WAS USED IN BOTH THE KITCHEN AND THE DINING ROOM.

Inlaid patterns resembling encaustic tile were produced using a stencil method in which different-colored granules were sprinkled into shaped perforated trays, after which the trays were removed and the sheets run through the rollers to fuse them. In 1898, Walton invented a process for making straight-line inlaid linoleum, which produced crisp geometric designs. In this process, strips of uncured linoleum were cut and pieced like a quilt before being calendered. Embossed inlaid linoleum, usually found in tile-like patterns, was introduced in 1926.

Those who couldn't afford linoleum used floorcloths or oilcloth: canvas that had been primed, painted, and coated with varnish. It was either cut to fit the shape of the kitchen and secured along the edges with tacks or hemmed and used as a rug over wooden flooring. Oilcloth was also popular as a table cover.

Another kind of resilient flooring was introduced in 1910: a bitumen-impregnated felt paper with a printed design on the face. This gave rise to many advertisements in period magazines urging consumers "for your own protection, learn how to tell genuine linoleum: look for the woven burlap back." The designs were similar to linoleum, and this product was especially popular as a rug, though it was also installed wall-to-wall. It didn't wear as well as linoleum because the pattern was only on the surface, whereas linoleum patterns go all the way through. If your old sheet flooring shows black patches in the worn areas, it is likely to be this material.

Some who could afford it used tile flooring. Small 1-inch mosaics or hexagonal tiles were the most common, sometimes with a simple border. Quarry tiles (6- or 8-inch squares) were also used. Tiles were either unglazed or had a matte glaze so they would not be slippery. Like countertop tile, floor tile was laid on a mortar bed, commonly known as a "mud job." The drawbacks of tile were commented on at the time and are the same today: it is hard on the feet, noisy, and things dropped on it are more likely to break. On the other hand, a good tile job will last practically forever.

Less common but seen occasionally were rubber floor tiles, cork tiles, and terrazzo. Rubber tiles were introduced in the early 1920s. Available in solid colors or marbleized designs, they were generally laid in a checkerboard pattern, were much more expensive than linoleum, so were more

likely to be found in wealthy homes or commercial businesses. Cork tiles, though introduced in 1899, did not gain acceptance till the 1920s when additives made them more impervious to water, grease, food, and dirt. Use of cork tiles was not widespread because of the limited color palette (varying shades of brown). Terrazzo floors (small pieces of stone set in a cement bed that is ground and polished) were introduced in the United States in 1890, but only after the invention around 1910 of electric grinders for polishing did terrazzo gain acceptance. While mentioned as a flooring material for kitchens in period magazines, it would have been an expensive floor at the time, limiting it to the homes of the wealthy. Like rubber tile, it was and is more likely to be found in commercial applications.

Stone floors were extremely rare, so it's best not to consider this medium.

Obsessive Restoration

Softwood floors were usually 1 x 4-inch tongue-and-groove fir or heart pine or some other inexpensive (at the time) local softwood. This type of flooring is still available but expensive. Hardwood floors were usually oak or maple. An existing wood floor can be sanded and refinished, or it can be painted. A floor sander will also remove existing paint. A floor with extensive water damage may have black stains caused by a chemical reaction between tannins in the wood and iron from the nails; neither sanding nor bleaching will remove these stains. Either shellac or varnish was used as a finish. Keep in mind that shellac doesn't resist water very well and varnish should be semigloss or satin. For a painted floor, oil-based enamel should be used. If the floor is used as both subfloor and finish floor, you may want to insulate underneath it.

Linoleum is still available, although only in solid colors, swirling marble, or vaguely granite-like patterns. It comes in sheets or as tiles (either 12 x 12-inch or approximately 2-foot squares). The marble patterns are unsurpassed at hiding dirt, handy for less-than-perfect housekeepers. Professional installation is recommended for sheet linoleum;

allowances must be made for its tendency to shrink. Be sure the installer is experienced with linoleum; it is not the same as installing vinyl. Professional installers can also put in inlaid borders or other designs, but keep it simple. Linoleum should end at the baseboard, rather than being coved (run a few inches up onto the wall). Tiles are a possible do-it-yourself installation, and they can also be cut up to make simple or more elaborate designs. Refrain from putting in a solid black-and-white checkerboard floor—all dirt that does not show up on the white tiles shows up on the black tiles. Early linoleum was often installed directly over the subfloor, which resulted in buckling and cracking of the linoleum because of seasonal wood movement. To remedy this, a felt underlay was glued to the subfloor first. With a plywood subfloor, this will not be a problem.

Existing ceramic tile should be restored, if possible. It will be difficult, though not completely impossible, to find matching tiles to replace broken or damaged ones. Sometimes the damage isn't too bad, and perhaps you can live with it. Small gouges can be patched with white thin-set mortar and touched up with paint or nail polish. If matching tiles cannot be found, try to figure out a way to incorporate new tiles into the design in a way that looks like it was done deliberately; otherwise, the patch will be obvious.

New ceramic tile should be installed only if there is existing tile that is beyond saving or if the house is elaborate enough that tile would have been an option for the original owner. (Bear in mind that the very wealthy would not have lavished much attention on the kitchen.) To be authentic, it should be installed on a mortar bed. (On the other hand, it will be impossible to tell by looking whether it's a "mud job" or cement board.) Unglazed tiles will need to be sealed. Tiles larger than 8 x 8 inches should be avoided, as they look too modern. Darker grout is acceptable for floors, but don't use such obviously modern colors as teal or purple.

Floorcloths are also an alternative. Many crafts books and magazines have directions for making them, or you can purchase them from artists. Making your own, however, would be in the fine tradition of the Arts & Crafts movement. Period floorcloths were very simple, either solid color or with a very simple design such as a checkerboard or tile pattern. A simple Arts & Crafts stencil design is not out of place as a border or an all-over pattern, or try a fabulous 1920s linoleum design.

Compromise Solution

Oak-strip flooring is presently cheaper than tongue-and-groove softwood and is an acceptable compromise. Either softwood or hardwood can be finished with a Swedish finish (preferred) or even polyurethane. Oil-based paint is best for a painted floor: it will hold up better in a kitchen. Laminate flooring is not acceptable—it does not look like wood; it looks like plastic.

As noted before, many old linoleum patterns are still being produced in vinyl, but the problem with modern vinyl is that it is too shiny: even a waxed and buffed linoleum floor is not as shiny as no-wax vinyl. There are a few vinyl patterns with a matte finish, though not many. A good compromise is commercial vinyl tile (the kind that's on the floor at the supermarket): it has a vaguely mottled pattern, is not shiny, and can be laid in a checkerboard for a fairly authentic look. It comes in some interesting colors, and cutting the 12 x 12-inch tiles into smaller squares can give an even more period look. It's also inexpensive. It's quite brittle when cold so make sure the subfloor is perfectly flat: it will crack over a ridge and will "telegraph" any bumps or nail heads. The self-stick vinyl tiles available have the same problem as their sheet-vinyl counterparts (i.e., too shiny and inappropriate patterns). Keep in mind also that real linoleum is about the same price as the better vinyl. Commercial-sheet vinyl is another possibility, as it tends to be less shiny and comes in some linoleum-like granite patterns. There is also a vinyl pattern that imitates 1-inch hexagonal tile quite convincingly. It is available only from Linoleum City in Hollywood (see Resources).

If ceramic tile is appropriate, laying it on cement board with thin-set mortar is fine, but stick to the same kinds of tile: mosaic, hexagon, or quarry tile.

CEILINGS, NOTHING MORE THAN CEILINGS

Walls and ceilings were mostly made of smooth-finish plaster over wood lath, then painted with enamel. Kitchen ceilings were usually the same height as the rest of the house, typically 8 to 10 feet. "The ceiling should be connected by a plain cove, never a molded cornice," wrote one expert in 1906, although the wall and ceiling often met at right angles. Sometimes the entire wall was plastered; other times the upper wall and ceiling were plastered, while the bottom part of the wall consisted of wooden wainscoting, either bead board or board-and-batten or ceramic tile. To save money, the plaster could be scored to look like tile and was sometimes finished with a glaze over the paint to make it look more tile-like.

Some authorities at the time felt that wood wainscoting was not "sanitary," but apparently that did not stop many builders from installing it. Occasionally the entire room was finished in bead board, though this was more common in utility areas and porches. Usually the bead board ran vertically, but in some areas of the country it was applied horizontally. Ceilings were also made of wooden board-and-batten on occasion (this was more common in rural areas). Tin ceilings belonged more to the Victorian era. A few period illustrations showed kitchens with a skylight in the ceiling, but this was quite rare in reality. Obviously the skylight was made of wire glass, not a modern plastic bubble.

COVED CEILINGS, WHILE NOT UNHEARD OF IN KITCHENS, ARE FAIRLY RARE. THESE ARE BEAUTIFULLY INTEGRATED WITH THE CABINETRY. THE ISLAND IS NEW, AND THE FLOOR HAS YET TO BE LAID.

Wallpaper was stripped from this wall in a butler's pantry, and the plaster underneath was painted a soft yellow that contrasts with the white trim and mahogany countertop.

There was a tendency for wood trim to be simpler in the kitchen than in the rest of the house, though not always. Door and window trim ran to 4 or 5 inches wide, with 5- to 7-inch baseboards. Windows were recommended to be set higher on the wall than elsewhere in the house, "so as to be above the sink and tables." Sometimes a 1 x 4-inch chair rail ran around the room on top of the plaster wall. Wood wainscoting, usually 4 feet high, was also topped by a chair rail. Wainscoting usually ran all the way around the room, even behind the cabinets, where it formed a backsplash. Some kitchens even had picture molding. And picture molding was also used as a crown molding on the upper cabinets.

Kitchen walls and ceilings were always painted with enamel for ease of cleaning, even if wainscoting and cabinets were varnished. Colors ran to off-white, cream, ivory, or beige. More color was recommended in the 1920s, but it still tended to be pastels such as green, gray, pink, blue, or yellow. Earlier kitchens (1900–1920) were usually all one color (some variation of white), while later kitchens (1920–1940) may have had more colors, although white still predominated. Two-color schemes, in which the wall was one color and the wainscoting and trim a different color, were fairly common. Some magazines recommended stenciled borders and such, but not too many people actually went to the trouble. Wallpaper was not often used in kitchens because it was difficult to keep clean, although a few periodicals recommended coating it with varnish to make it washable. Oilcloth was used as a wallcovering occasionally. Specialty wallcoverings called "sanitaries" were available but were much less common than paint.

Obsessive Restoration

Plaster has a handcrafted look and a slight unevenness that is hard to duplicate with drywall. Existing plaster that is cracked or damaged can be patched, and sagging plaster can sometimes be reattached with plaster washers. If the plaster is too far gone, the room will have to be replastered. The unbelievably obsessive, or maybe those restoring a house museum, will use wooden lath, but otherwise expanded metal lath is fine. An acceptable alternative is skim-coat plaster over blueboard (special water-resistant drywall). Here are some 1906 directions for faux tile:

When nearly dry, [plaster] should be lightly marked off with a mason's jointing tool into squares, and later, if desired, painted with four coats of paint, the last being of the best white enamel.

Painting with oil-based enamel is still an option. When painting an existing kitchen, be sure to clean thoroughly with TSP first. The substance formed by grease combined with the by-products of gas combustion is very hard to remove. Avoid really bright whites, which were not available in the early part of the century. Stick with ivory, cream, beige, pale yellow, etc. Faux tile can receive a glazed topcoat over the paint for a more tile-like look. Consult books on decorative painting for techniques, but remember that fancy glazed finishes would not be appropriate.

Varnished woodwork or wainscoting was usually finished with shellac. (To test for this, dip a cotton swab in denatured alcohol and test in an inconspicuous place; if the finish dissolves, it's shellac.) Shellac tends to darken and crack with age, but it strips off easily with denatured alcohol or ammonia. Shellac is sensitive to water and alcohol, so it isn't the most practical finish; but a few coats of shellac with a topcoat of varnish will give the right look with a little more durability.

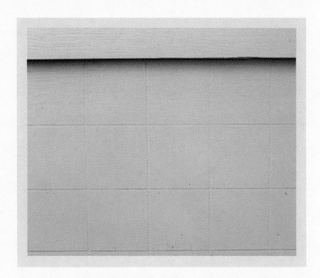

A PATTERN OF 4¼ X 4¼-INCH TILES HAS BEEN INCISED INTO THIS PLASTER WAINSCOTING AND THEN PAINTED. SOMETIMES THIS FAUX TILE WAS GIVEN A GLAZED PAINT FINISH TO MAKE IT LOOK MORE LIKE CERAMIC TILE.

Compromise Solution

Most people will not notice the difference between drywall and lath-and-plaster. It is a particularly good solution for a badly cracked ceiling: just put up a layer of ¼-inch or ⅜-inch drywall right over the plaster. Skim-coated drywall will look a little more plaster-like. The drywall should have a smooth finish: avoid spray texture or that dreadful texture they use in office buildings and modern houses. It should still be possible to do a faux-tile finish even with skim-coated drywall.

Latex semigloss is perfectly reasonable for painting walls or ceilings. The same color choices would tend to apply (off-white to pastels). Varnish or spar varnish is good for unpainted woodwork or wainscoting. Polyurethane looks too much like plastic.

PANE AND FANCY

By the twentieth century, the days of the kitchen in a windowless basement were over. Most authorities recommended a kitchen have windows on two sides for cross-ventilation, and some builders actually did this. Casement windows were thought to provide better ventilation (which they do), but either casements or double-hung windows were installed. Other window styles such as awning, hopper, and sliding windows rarely put in an appearance. Windows were generally made of wood, either varnished or painted, except in house styles such as Tudor Revival where metal casements were common. It was considered a good idea for the windows to be set high enough to fit counters or tables underneath.

They were still very door-happy in the Arts & Crafts period, perhaps a Victorian holdover. Some kitchens had four, five, or even more doors. Most of them were identical in style to the doors in the rest of the house, although frequently the door to the dining room was a swinging door, sometimes with a window. The back door generally had a

Obsessive Restoration

The obsessive restorer will of course leave all the existing doors and windows, no matter how inconvenient. Sometimes only the door itself is inconvenient and can be removed, leaving the opening intact. The spring-loaded hardware on swinging doors will benefit from a squirt of lubricant. Try to avoid removing a swinging door; they are difficult to re-hang. (If you're having trouble fitting the fridge through the door, take the doors off the fridge instead.) Back doors usually had one large window at the top, although eight- or ten-light single French doors are also frequently found. Doors like this are still available, as are the wooden screen doors that go with them. Screen doors should be hung on spring hinges so they close properly. Hook-and-eyes were used to fasten them shut. Wooden windows, especially double-hung windows, often suffer from broken sash cords or from being painted shut but are easily repaired. Rotted sashes can also be replaced. If the windows are not set high enough for a counter and if more counter space is needed, they can be shortened (either using carpentry and shorter sashes or with new complete window units). Completely new windows will probably have to meet current code, which in most places means at least double-glazing. Double-glazed windows look different in subtle ways from old windows, so keep that in mind. Skylights were rare but useful for bringing light to a dark kitchen. A wire-glass skylight will be harder to find and may cause problems with the building inspector, so do some research before deciding on the solution.

Compromise Solution

The architect, kitchen designer, or contractor will want to remove several doorways "to open up the space." Try to resist. Take out only doors or windows that make absolutely no sense. If replacement windows are being used, try to match the muntin pattern (or lack thereof) to the other windows in the house. An entire wall (or two) of windows will look much too modern: a row of three will be plenty. And windows in the backsplash, transoms above the tops of the cabinets, or other openings from the kitchen onto a porch, patio, or deck seem to be the style these days. Try to make them very simple and plain: no sidelights, transoms, art glass, etc. Skylights are another (often unnecessary) item professionals seem to favor. If the kitchen is very dark and there is no other way to increase the amount of light, a skylight can be helpful. Because multiple skylights look very modern, it is better to have one larger one. Avoid the plastic bubble skylights by using the flat "roof window" type.

window, or a multi-light French door was occasionally found. And the back door always had a wooden screen door to keep out insects during the warmer months. As with wooden windows, doors were either varnished or painted. Keep in mind that for all the talk about "bringing the outdoors in" during this period, they were not talking about the backyard, which was considered more of a utility area for hanging laundry and growing a vegetable garden. In most bungalows the way to the backyard is through the utility porch. Double French doors leading out onto a porch or terrace were generally reserved for the living room or dining room.

OPPOSITE: FIVE LARGE DOUBLE-HUNG WINDOWS BRING A GENEROUS AMOUNT OF LIGHT INTO THIS NEW KITCHEN, AS WELL AS VIEWS OF THE BACKYARD. THE KITCHEN IS LARGE ENOUGH THAT UPPER CABINET STORAGE SPACE COULD BE SACRIFICED FOR THE LARGER WINDOWS, SOMETHING NOT TRUE IN THE AVERAGE BUNGALOW. A WOODEN-TOPPED ISLAND WITH STORAGE AT ONE END AND A TABLE AT THE OTHER ANCHORS THE MIDDLE OF THE ROOM. STRUCTURAL BEAMS WERE GIVEN A HAND-HEWN LOOK AND STAINED. EIGHT PENDANT FIXTURES PROVIDE AMPLE ILLUMINATION WITH AN APPROPRIATE PERIOD LOOK, UNLIKE THE UBIQUITOUS RECESSED CANS THAT SEEM TO BE THE CURRENT FAD.

CHEAP FRILLS

Although the kitchen was mainly considered a workroom, there was still some attempt to make it cheerful and pleasant. Even in the era when white was predominant, walls were occasionally painted in such colors as yellow or pink, and once in a while stencil designs were added. Wallpaper was not common, unless it was varnished, but printed oilcloth was applied to walls. Linoleum added color and pattern underfoot. Sometimes cabinets were painted in a two-tone look, or glass-fronted cabinets were etched or stenciled. Color was especially prevalent in the 1920s. Flowers or pots of herbs were thought to be appropriate windowsill decorations. Dish towels were often embroidered or appliquéd with designs (fruits, vegetables, animals, and days of the week were popular). Rugs or mats were used in front of the sink and other work areas. Simple rod-pocket or cafe curtains of muslin, voile, and dotted swiss covered the windows. Some authors of the time felt that art was inappropriate, but that didn't stop anyone from hanging prints, calendars, and the like on the limited wall space. There were decorative match-safes, flue covers with artistic scenes printed on them, and of course, the wondrous variety of artistic tins, cans, and boxes for the new packaged foods that were becoming available. Step-on waste cans, enameled in various colors, found a place beneath the sink. Sets of tables and chairs made especially for kitchens and breakfast nooks could be purchased (the forerunner of the dinette set), and a porcelain-top table was a common kitchen fixture. And no kitchen would be complete without a clock for keeping track of cooking times.

OPPOSITE: A COLLECTION OF OLD KITCHENWARE, PACKAGING, DEPRESSION GLASS, CANISTERS, AND VINTAGE DISHTOWELS DECORATE THIS 1920S KITCHEN REMODEL IN A VICTORIAN HOUSE. ■■ RIGHT: LACE EDGING DECORATES THE ADJUSTABLE SHELVES IN THIS BUTLER'S PANTRY, WHERE THE CHINA HAS BEEN ARRANGED IN A PLEASING MANNER. A SMALL SINK FOR WASHING UP HAS A HINGED DRAINBOARD THAT CAN BE FOLDED AGAINST THE WALL. IT WAS BELIEVED TO BE UNSANITARY TO WASH CHINA, GLASS, AND UTENSILS IN THE KITCHEN; ONLY COOKING POTS AND SUCH WERE WASHED THERE.

Obsessive Restoration

Many wonderful vintage kitchen items can be found at reasonable prices through antiques dealers, yard sales, and thrift stores. Old packaging is an especially nice touch, and some products retain their historic packaging to this day (Kingsford's Cornstarch and Calumet Baking Powder, for instance). Vintage appliances like toasters and waffle irons often work better than their modern counterparts. Utensils, cookware, and gadgets are still decorative as well as useful. Such textiles as tablecloths, napkins, dish towels, pot holders, and curtains can be used to add color and pattern. Simple rod-pocket curtains can be purchased at department and specialty stores; for those who sew, they can be made easily and inexpensively. There are endless possibilities for the truly obsessed: period mousetraps, ice cards, eggbeaters, salt and pepper shakers, soap savers.

Compromise Solution

Keeping in mind that there were no refrigerator magnets, there is still room for expression in kitchen decor. Prints, posters, calendars, or framed art tiles can decorate walls. There is no lack of colorful dish towels, pot holders, and napkins, as well as utensils, decorative canisters, or interesting bottles. While there were no mini-blinds at the time, shutters would be an acceptable substitute, and lace curtains, though unlikely to be found in a period kitchen, do a fine job of softening the light and disguising an unattractive view. Rugs or mats were usually placed at the work areas, and an Oriental rug doesn't really look out of place in a kitchen.

A STENCILED BORDER WAS ADDED TO THE CREAM-COLORED BEAD-BOARD WALLS OF THIS KITCHEN. A TILED COUNTER WITH A WOODEN EDGE TOPS NEW LOWER CAB-INETS OF DOUGLAS FIR WITH BRASS HARDWARE.

A 1916 BUNGALOW IN A RURAL SMALL TOWN SPORTS UNUSUAL STENCILED AND BACK-PAINTED GLASS CABINET DOORS. VINTAGE CALENDARS AND PRINTS DECORATE THE WALLS, AND THE WINDOWSILL HOLDS A COPPER TRAY FULL OF POTTED PLANTS, AS RECOMMENDED BY MANY PERIOD MAGAZINES. THE ORIGINAL WOODEN COUNTERTOP IS STILL IN PLACE, THOUGH IT HAS BEGUN TO DETERIORATE AROUND THE SINK. THE BOARD-AND-BATTEN WALLS AND CEILINGS WERE MORE OFTEN FOUND IN COUNTRY HOMES. A FUNCTIONING CRANK WALL PHONE COMPLETES THE SCENE. ■■ CLOSE-UP OF THE STENCIL AND BACK-PAINTING ON GLASS CABINET DOORS.

THE WINDOW ON THE LEFT WAS SHORTENED TO MATCH THE WINDOW ON THE
RIGHT, ALLOWING FOR MORE COUNTER SPACE (PREVIOUSLY THE SILL OF THE
LEFT-HAND WINDOW SAT 18 INCHES ABOVE THE FLOOR). ALMOND-COLORED TILE
WITH A WOODEN EDGE TREATMENT TOPS NEW CABINETS WITH INSET DRAWERS.
THE BEAD-BOARD WAINSCOT CONTINUES BEHIND THE CABINETS TO FORM A BACK-
SPLASH. A REBUILT COOLER CABINET SITS TO THE RIGHT OF THE SINK.

THE BUTLER'S PANTRY IN THIS 1910 HOUSE HAS OPEN SHELVING AS WELL AS CABINETS. THE MAHOGANY COUNTER AT LEFT REPLACED A WOOD-GRAIN LAMINATE COUNTER PUT IN BY PREVIOUS OWNERS; THE PAINTED COUNTER IS LIKELY MAHOGANY UNDERNEATH.

A CORNER CABINET WITH A LEADED-GLASS DOOR IS ONE OF TWO IN THE BREAKFAST ROOM OF THIS 1931 TUDOR, WHERE IT DISPLAYS SOME OF THE OWNER'S COLLECTION OF VINTAGE DINNERWARE. GREEN OR OTHER COLORED GLASS KNOBS WERE POPULAR IN THE 1920S AND 1930S. ▪▪ RIGHT: THE SHELVES IN THIS BUTLER'S PANTRY WEAR ROYAL EDGE–BRAND PAPER EDGING PRINTED WITH FRUITS AND VEGETABLES (PROBA-BLY FROM THE 1950S). THE WINDOW ON THE RIGHT ALLOWS LIGHT FROM AN ADJACENT BREAKFAST ROOM TO ENTER THE SPACE. THE UPPER DOOR ON THE LEFT IS PART OF THE COOLER CABINET AND ONCE HAD GLASS IN IT LIKE THE OTHERS.

THIS COOLER CABINET (SOMETIMES CALLED A "CALIFORNIA COOLER") IS LOCATED ON AN INSIDE WALL AND VENTED TO THE ATTIC AND BASEMENT. BY PROVIDING STORAGE FOR FOODS THAT NEEDED TO BE KEPT COOL BUT NOT REFRIGERATED, THESE CABINETS FREED UP VALUABLE SPACE IN THE ICEBOX FOR MORE PERISHABLE FOODS. NEXT TO IT IS ONE OF TWO TILT-OUT BINS.

THE OAK HOOSIER CABINET IN THIS 1915 KITCHEN HAS A ZINC WORK SURFACE THAT PULLS OUT. ON THE LEFT IS THE FLOUR SIFTER, A STANDARD FEATURE, AND ON THE RIGHT, A TAMBOUR DOOR, WHICH COULD BE PULLED DOWN TO HIDE SOME OF THE MESS. ON THE WORK SURFACE ARE VARIOUS PIECES OF KITCHEN EQUIPMENT, INCLUDING THE GREEN-PEA SHELLER ON THE FRONT CORNER. BEHIND THE CABINET ARE THE BACK STAIRS USED BY THE SERVANTS.

HERE IS A TRULY STUNNING TILE INSTALLATION IN A 1931 TUDOR. THE SQUARE MOSAIC TILE ON THE COUNTER IS HIGHLIGHTED BY LINES OF GOLD TILES THAT MATCH THE EDGING AND THE QUARTER-ROUND TILES AROUND THE SINK. THE MATCHING GREEN SUBWAY TILE ON THE BACKSPLASH HAS A GOLD LINER STRIP INTERSPERSED WITH SMALL BLACK SQUARES, WHICH STEPS UP ONE TILE UNDERNEATH THE CABINETS. A RECESSED SPACE FOR A SPONGE AND A SOAP DISH (UNFORTUNATELY BROKEN OFF) ALSO HAVE A GOLD GLAZE. BLACK HEXAGONAL CABINET KNOBS ECHO THE BLACK SQUARES IN THE LINER.

ABOVE: A NEW BACKSPLASH AND SOAPSTONE COUNTER COVERS CABINETS WITH OVERLAY DRAWER FRONTS THAT HAVE A ROUTED-EDGE DETAIL, COMMON IN CABINETS FROM THE 1920S. LEFT: THIS SOAPSTONE COUNTER HAS GROOVES FOR DRAINAGE. (PHOTOS COURTESY OF VICTORIA MAKER)

Baker's tables like this one were one of the first forms of what we now know as islands. Two drawers and two bins provided more storage than a typical worktable. Next to the table is a Smoothtop-brand stove (and the top is smooth) with gas cocks and exposed piping.

FREESTANDING CABINETS LIKE THIS ONE AT ARDENWOOD HISTORIC FARM IN FREMONT, CALIFORNIA, ARE SOMEWHAT UNUSUAL. IT HAS A TYPICAL ARRANGEMENT OF DRAWERS, TILT-OUT BINS, AND DOORS, AS WELL AS A PINE TOP, WHICH DISPLAYS A VARIETY OF VINTAGE KITCHEN EQUIPMENT. THERE IS EVEN AN ANTIQUE MOUSETRAP ON THE FLOOR NEAR THE LEFT LEG. A CABINET LIKE THIS WOULD BE A GOOD SOLUTION FOR THOSE WHO FEEL THEY NEED TOE-KICK SPACE, WHICH MOST PERIOD CABINETS DON'T HAVE.

A TYPICAL 1920S TILE INSTALLATION OF 2-INCH HEXAGONAL TILES WITH A CONTRASTING EDGE TILE HAS AN UNUSUAL SUBWAY TILE BACKSPLASH. GENERALLY SUBWAY TILE WAS LAID IN RUNNING BOND LIKE BRICKS RATHER THAN WITH THE JOINTS MATCHING UP. A TILE-IN SINK IS ALMOST ALWAYS SURROUNDED BY QUARTER-ROUND TILES THAT MATCH THE FIELD TILE OR THE EDGING. RECESSED AREAS FOR SOAP OR SPONGES WERE USUALLY INCLUDED. A LIGHT FIXTURE WITH A HAND-PAINTED SHADE HANGS OVER THE SINK.

H EXAGONAL GLASS KNOBS AND BRIDGE HANDLES ON THE DRAWERS WERE ALSO POPULAR, BOTH CLEAR AND IN COLORS. THE CABINET ON THE RIGHT CONCEALS A
DISHWASHER. ABOVE THE WINDOWS IS AN ELECTRIC VENTILATOR. THREE SIMPLE PENDANT LIGHTS ILLUMINATE THE AREA.

These new cabinets have a different take on the usual Shaker doors yet are still within the realm of appropriate cabinets. Even the angled corner cabinets might have been found in an early kitchen. ∎∎ Right: A large pantry cabinet shows typical doors and inset drawers with glass knobs, bridge handles, and nickel hinges. A simple crown molding tops the cabinets.

These fir cabinets have a dark stain that approximates the color of eighty-year-old shellac. They have the usual hardware but lack the visible hinges that a period cabinet would have.

Paint in the pores of the wood indicates that this cabinet door was originally painted. An easy way to remove the remaining paint is to put on a coat of shellac, then strip it off. The shellac sticks to the paint and pulls it out of the pores.

■■ Right: These original cabinets were the victims of a 1950s facelift. Plywood slab doors and a boomerang-patterned laminate countertop were added. New frame-and-panel doors, drawer fronts, and a new countertop could bring this kitchen back to its original self.

LEFT: CABINETS IN THIS NEW BUTLER'S PANTRY ARE MADE WITH PLYWOOD DOOR PANELS AND MODERN JOINERY YET STILL RETAIN AN OLD LOOK BECAUSE OF THEIR BEAD-BOARD BACKS AND MORTISED HINGES. ■■ ABOVE: CABINETS IN THIS BUNGALOW ARE PAINTED A CREAMY YELLOW THAT HARMONIZES WITH THE MAPLE COUNTERTOP. A REFURBISHED 1940S STOVE GLEAMS IN THE BACKGROUND.

This worktable at the Gamble House in Pasadena very much resembles a modern island. It is unusual in that the drawers can be pulled out from either side.

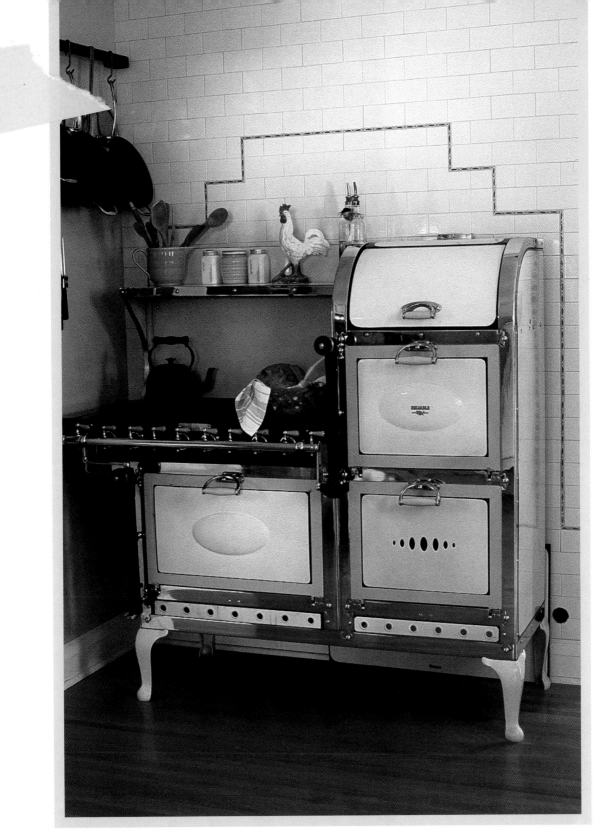

THE DECORATIVE LINER STRIP IN THIS TILED WALL HAS BEEN STEPPED UP TO FRAME THE REFURBISHED STOVE. A FULLY TILED WALL WAS LESS COMMON THAN A TILE WAINSCOT, MAINLY DUE TO THE EXPENSE.

A BUILT-IN IRONING BOARD FOLDS OUT OF A CABINET IN THIS 1931 HOUSE. NEXT TO IT IS A METAL-LINED STORAGE COM-
PARTMENT, ALLOWING THE IRON TO BE PUT AWAY WHILE STILL HOT.

Clockwise from top: A microwave hides in a cabinet with a lift-up door. Below, a pull-out cutting board provides a place to put the food before or after heating it. ▪▪ The dishwasher hides in this island yet is still convenient to the sink (not shown), which is just across the aisle to the right. ▪▪ A tilt-out tray under the sink for dishwashing supplies is not just a modern invention. Many original kitchens have something similar.

THIS NEW PANTRY CABINET IS MADE FROM VERTICAL-GRAIN DOUGLAS FIR
WITH A CLEAR FINISH. THE DESIGN OF THE CABINET IS REMINISCENT OF
THE OTHER BUILT-INS IN THIS 1911 HOUSE.

A NOTHER FREESTANDING CABINET IN THE SAME HOUSE INCLUDES A MARBLE
COUNTER. NOTE THE HIGH SUBWAY-TILED WAINSCOT.

Appliances

In many ways, the invention of appliances for cooking, refrigeration, and cleaning is what drove the evolution of the modern kitchen. Without advances in the technology of appliances, other innovations such as continuous countertops or the concept of the work triangle would be almost meaningless.

HOME ON THE RANGE

After initial resistance, wood- and coal-burning cookstoves and ranges gained wide acceptance in the late nineteenth century. The first gas stove was

If you're going to have an old stove, it might as well be red, like this 1910 Eureka model. Four burners on the right are gas fired, while the four on the left burn wood.

A CLASSIC WOOD/GAS WEDGEWOOD FROM THE 1930S SITS ON THE ORIGINAL INLAID LINOLEUM IN THIS KITCHEN. PORCELAIN CASTERS UNDER THE FEET PREVENT PERMANENT DENTS IN THE FLOOR. THE WOODBURNING PART IS UNDER THE TEAKETTLE; ON THE RIGHT ARE THE OVEN AND BROILER. THE DRAWER IN THE CENTER IS FOR STORAGE.

introduced in 1879, and by the 1890s it was in wide use in urban areas where gas was readily available. Oil-burning stoves were also available, although some found the smell objectionable. Wood- or coal-burning stoves had the drawback of heating up the room, which was fine in winter but undesirable in summer. (In warmer climates, this led to the development of the "summer kitchen," a separate room away from the house where cooking was done in the summer months.) Many manufacturers offered combination coal/gas or wood/gas stoves for this reason, and those who had the space and the money might have had two stoves in their kitchen: a coal- or wood-burning one for winter and a gas- or oil-burning one for summer.

Victorian-era stoves were often built into a brick-lined niche (or even an existing fireplace), but after the turn of the twentieth century, stoves were more likely to be freestanding. Wood or coal stoves were placed a safe distance from the wall, backing up to a chimney for the flue pipe and often surrounded by tiled walls and flooring. Gas stoves might also be placed in a tiled niche or, because they didn't need the same level of fireproofing, could be freestanding (though a flue was still required).

A hot-water tank was usually connected to the stove to heat water. (If you still have a hot-water heater in your kitchen, this is why.) Later this was sometimes replaced by an instant hot-water heater in the basement or kitchen. Some of these were quite beautiful with cast Art Nouveau patterns in the housing. If you still have a functioning instant heater, by all means keep it. Stoves were usually made of cast iron or

A SMALL HOTPOINT ELECTRIC STOVE WAS ADDED IN A 1928 KITCHEN REMODEL AT THE BENNETT RANCH IN LAKE FOREST, CALIFORNIA. NEAR IT IS A PORCELAIN-TOPPED KITCHEN TABLE WITH MATCHING CHAIRS—THE FORERUNNER OF THE DINETTE SET.

sheet steel with decorative nickel plating. After the turn of the century, porcelain enamel stoves were produced. They were easier to keep clean and did not need continuing applications of stove-black. Electric stoves were available by the 1920s but did not become popular until the 1930s.

Early gas stoves were fairly primitive, with exposed gas piping and industrial-looking gas cocks. They lacked insulation and thermostats. While woodstoves tended to be boxy, gas stoves usually had cabriole-style legs. By the 1920s and 1930s, gas stoves started to be more enclosed, though the legs remained. Advances in porcelain enamel led to stoves in various colors, even marbleized finishes, though

most porcelain stoves were white or ivory (not unlike today). The invention of the oven thermostat made baking easier. Stoves took on a more Deco look in the 1930s, and toward the 1940s the legs began to shorten, leading to a mere suggestion of legs by the late 1940s and early 1950s. Eventually, legs disappeared from view altogether. Beginning in the 1920s, stoves also began to sprout clocks, salt and pepper shakers, shelves, lights, griddles, and so forth.

Obsessive Restoration

Although it is true that a wood-fired oven results in a much better crust on your baked goods, unless you are living "off-the-grid" or you have a house museum, I would not recommend a wood cookstove as a full-time stove. There is also air pollution to consider. However, if you want to go that way, both antique and reproduction wood-burning stoves are still available, as are antique and reproduction gas and electric stoves. Since stoves are basically very simple, antique stoves are easily repaired and restored, and parts are available. Many older gas stoves did not have pilot lights and had to be lit with matches, but later models (from the teens on) had pilot lights as well as oven thermostats, which were initially an expensive option that was not available on all stoves. Combination wood/coal and gas stoves may cause some building inspectors to insist on a double or triple wall flue on the off chance that you might possibly burn wood or coal, so be prepared. Electric stoves were never as popular as gas, so availability of antique electric models is limited. A fully restored double-oven model will be fairly expensive, but you can still find antique stoves in good condition through the want ads, at garage/estate sales, or even at used-appliance outlets for a fairly reasonable price. In stoves, an antique generally looks better than a reproduction, which tends to have modern-looking burners.

No discussion of stoves would be complete without mentioning appropriate cookware. Cast iron, of course, has been in use for a very long time, is still produced, and is entirely appropriate for a period kitchen. It can be handed down to your children. In fact, my grandmother's cast-iron skillets are still being used by my mother. Graniteware first became available in the 1880s and is still available today. It gained wide acceptance because it was easy to clean and weighed far less than cast iron. Aluminum cookware was first introduced in the 1890s, but it was expensive and inferior to graniteware at the time. Improvements were made by 1910, and sales of aluminum cookware increased. Pyrex oven-

A 1940s-ERA O'KEEFE AND MERRITT STOVE IS NOTEWORTHY FOR THE GLASS WINDOW ON THE RIGHT: AN ANGLED MIRROR INSIDE ALLOWS THE INSIDE OF THE OVEN TO BE VIEWED WITHOUT OPENING THE DOOR.

ware was introduced in 1915 and immediately became popular because it was easy to clean and also economical because baking could be done at lower temperatures. White enamelware with accent colors like red or green became popular in the 1920s, along with colored handles on kitchen tools in red, green, yellow, blue, black, and white. Old cookware is easy to find through antiques dealers and garage sales and is relatively affordable. Stove-top glass cookware was introduced in 1936.

SOME VINTAGE COOKWARE IS SHOWN HERE IN THE KITCHEN OF THE LANTERMAN HOUSE IN LA CAÑADA–FLINTRIDGE, CALIFORNIA.

Compromise Solution

For some reason, any vintage stove, even one from the 1950s, seems to have the right "old" look for a period kitchen. It's as though the owners went out and bought a new stove every twenty years or so. Reproduction stoves from companies such as Heartland have the old look but with modern gas or electric burners and other modern features. Commercial-style stoves also have the sort of industrial aesthetic seen in some old stoves, although many ranges had quite elaborate decoration. Those with unlimited funds might want to consider the French La Cornue range (pretty much the Rolls-Royce of stoves) or the English Aga Cooker. The other option is a modern freestanding range. There were no cooktops or wall ovens, although there were apartment-size stoves that sat on the counter with the oven above. Even though period-looking wall ovens are available, they look phony.

THE ICEMAN COMETH

Although the ice chest was introduced in the 1860s, it was not until the 1880s that iceboxes came into general use. Iceboxes represented a monumental advance in storage for perishable foods, which previously could only be preserved by canning, smoking, salting, or storage in root cellars or springhouses. Iceboxes were the standard in most homes until the general introduction of electric refrigeration in the 1910s; before that it was limited to commercial use or the kitchens of the wealthy in places such as the Biltmore Estate in North Carolina. Either freestanding or built into the wall, iceboxes were placed in the kitchen, the pantry, or on the back porch. Usually made of hardwoods like oak or ash, they were first lined with metal or zinc and later with porcelain. Insulation (usually felt, cork, and charcoal) and dead air lined the space between the wood and the metal compartments. The wood was left natural or painted with enamel. A block of ice was placed in a compartment at the top, and cool air would waft downward over the food. As the ice melted, a tube directed the runoff to a drain or a drip pan (which had to be emptied regularly). An ice card left in the window notified the iceman how many pounds of ice should be left on any given day. Some iceboxes were built so ice could be delivered directly through a door that opened to the outside. In cold climates, this door could be left open in the winter, economizing on ice.

In 1927 General Electric introduced the now famous Monitor-Top Refrigerator, which immediately became a best-seller. An advertisement at the time read, "It is called the seven cubic foot size, but that gives you no indication of its vast shelf area . . . visualize a shelf one foot wide and twelve feet long . . . that's the real size of this seemingly small refrigerator." In 1927 the Maine Manufacturing Company advertised its White Mountain Stone White Deluxe Refrigerators, stating "four bolts at the top of the ice chamber provide for immediate or future installation of standard electrical refrigerating units." The refrigerator could be ordered "in colors to match the modern kitchen," including white, blue, gray, green, ivory, natural oak, or custom colors. By the 1930s electric refrigerators were standard equipment wherever electricity was available. Gas-powered refrigerators were also available and are still being made. Electric refrigerators, as with iceboxes, could be either freestanding or built-in. Built-in iceboxes or refrigerators (the terms were used interchangeably) sometimes had tiled or porcelain enamel fronts, although wood was probably more likely. Common to all refrigerators was heavy brass or nickel-plated hardware. Shelves were made of wire, glass, or porcelain-enameled metal.

A BUILT-IN ELECTRIC REFRIGERATOR MAY DATE TO 1909 WHEN THIS HOUSE WAS BUILT, OR IT MAY HAVE BEEN ADDED LATER. IT HAS BEEN RESTORED TO WORKING ORDER BY THE CURRENT OWNER. ■■ OPPOSITE: AND YOU THOUGHT THE SIDE-BY-SIDE REFRIGERATOR WAS A MODERN INVENTION. THIS MODEL, IN THE KITCHEN OF THE 1899 DUNSMUIR HOUSE IN OAKLAND, CALIFORNIA, PROBABLY DATES TO THE 1930S. IT SITS ON SOME CLASSIC CHECKED LINOLEUM OF ABOUT THE SAME VINTAGE.

IN 1931, THIS WAS THE BIGGEST WESTINGHOUSE REFRIGERATOR AVAILABLE. THE OWNERS OF THIS HOUSE SEARCHED A LONG TIME TO FIND THE TRIANGULAR BLACK COASTERS FOR THE FEET. THE KITCHEN IS A 1920S REMODEL IN A VICTORIAN HOUSE (NOTE THE STAINED-GLASS WINDOW). THE LOWER CABINETS HAVE SLAB DOORS, WHICH ARE LESS COMMON THAN FRAME AND PANEL BUT NOT WITHOUT PRECEDENT. THE LIGHT FIXTURE OVER THE SINK IS FITTED WITH A REPRODUCTION EDISON BULB. MANY OWNERS OF VINTAGE REFRIGERATORS ALSO KEEP A MODERN FROST-FREE MODEL STASHED ELSEWHERE, BUT WHEN THIS INQUIRY WAS MADE, WE WERE ESCORTED TO THE BACK PORCH TO SEE THE MODERN REFRIGERATOR, A 1940S FRIGIDAIRE.

Obsessive Restoration

It's awfully hard to get regular ice delivery these days, although it is still possible to pick up block ice fairly conveniently. However, antique iceboxes can be retrofitted with compressors for electric refrigeration. GE Monitor Tops and other antique refrigerators can still be found, though they are not as numerous as old stoves. Most of them used ammonia as a refrigerant until the invention of Freon in the thirties. The major drawback of antique refrigerators is their lack of space (particularly freezer space) and the necessity of defrosting regularly. So here is a defrosting tip, courtesy of my mother: once a week, unplug the refrigerator for six to eight hours—long enough to melt the frost build-up but not long enough to spoil the food. For ease, put the whole thing on a timer, and keep the door closed.

A side-by-side refrigerator with black handles disappears into a wall of stained Douglas-fir cabinetry. The butcher block–topped island has the dishwasher tucked under it. A vintage six-burner stove anchors the other side of the room.

Compromise Solution

The frost-free refrigerator has got to be one of the finer inventions of the twentieth century. There are several ways to integrate a modern refrigerator into a period kitchen, which fall into two categories: hiding it or not hiding it. If money is no object, there are refrigerator and freezer drawers that can be built into the cabinetry. Some European manufacturers make refrigerators that resemble armoires when closed. Separate refrigerator and freezer units can be used if layout allows. Many refrigerators are made to accept wood panels on the front, but the problem with this method is that the modern aluminum trim on the edges announces, "I'm a refrigerator with wood panels on the front!" No one is fooled. A better method is to cover the entire door with wood and have new wooden handles made, though even this will still say "refrigerator" because of the size of the doors (most cabinet doors are not thirty inches wide). Another possibility is to build the refrigerator into an alcove that can be closed off with doors or even with a curtain. If it wouldn't be too inconvenient, it can also be placed out on the utility porch or in the pantry. Avoid obviously modern facing materials such as stainless steel or black glass and stick with white or almond. On the other hand, if you're stuck with some dreadful harvest-gold model from the 1970s and you have to keep it, it might not be out of line to paint it some lovely Arts & Crafts color and add a faux finish or a stencil design, or you can use construction adhesive to glue wood or painted panels to the front. Not strictly period but probably an improvement.

LEFT: A MIELE DISHWASHER HAS ALL THE CONTROLS ON THE TOP EDGE, ALLOWING THE ENTIRE FRONT TO BE COVERED WITH A WOODEN PANEL THAT MATCHES THE CABINETRY. ■■ RIGHT: A BOARD-AND-BATTEN DOOR IN THE GREENE & GREENE STYLE OF THE MAIN ROBINSON HOUSE KITCHEN HIDES THE DISHWASHER IN THE NEW KITCHEN OF THE CARRIAGE HOUSE.

DISHING IT OUT

Washing dishes has got to be one of the most boring and repetitive of all kitchen tasks, so it's no wonder that with the advent of electricity the dishwasher soon followed. Dishwashers were being produced as early as the first decade of the twentieth century. Here is a description from *The Outlook* magazine in 1906: "Where large quantities of dishes must be washed, the work is now done by machinery. The dishes, piled in a wire basket suspended from a traveling crane, are lowered into violently agitating boiling soapsuds, which remove every particle of soil; in a few seconds they are plunged into a cauldron of clean boiling water, lifted, and left in the basket; when cool they are spotlessly bright." Undoubtedly this describes a commercial dishwasher, although the article mentions that small dishwashing machines for family use have recently been invented. The

first dishwashers were built into one bowl of a two-bowl sink. Eventually portable units that hooked up to the sink, similar to today's portable dishwashers, became the norm. These were round rather than square and similar in shape to old wringer-style washers. They loaded from the top. Though widely advertised, dishwashers were considered a luxury item (probably by men, who rarely did the dishes) and did not become widespread until after World War II, when the under-the-counter built-in dishwasher that is now standard was introduced.

The dishwasher is a convenient place to store the dirty dishes, freeing up the counter and the sink and keeping the mess out of sight. Although that function alone would be worthwhile, the fact that it will also wash the dishes is a bonus. Now if someone would invent a machine that would also put the dishes away . . .

When a full-size dishwasher won't fit, an 18-inch model (available from several manufacturers) may solve the problem. Except for the sink cabinet, which was made deeper for the dishwasher, all the other cabinets are original to the house. A checkerboard floor of commercial vinyl tile makes the narrow kitchen appear larger.

Obsessive Restoration

The likelihood of finding a functioning antique dishwasher is extremely small. If you have one, by all means keep it, if only as a conversation piece. More likely there will be no dishwasher at all. If you don't mind doing dishes by hand, then that will be no problem. You might consider building a dirty-dish closet, detailed in the cabinets section. If you do want a dishwasher, it will have to be hidden in some way.

Compromise Solution

The dishwasher is another truly fine invention of the twentieth century, and most people want one. There are various ways to integrate dishwashers into a period kitchen. It could be left out in the open (again, as with refrigerators, no one will be fooled by a wooden panel on the front). However, some expensive European models are available with all the controls on the top edge, allowing the entire front to be covered with a false front; a bank of three false drawers looks pretty good. The new "dishwasher drawers" manufactured by Fisher and Paykel also accept wooden fronts that match the other cabinetry. Another option is to make the cabinets a little deeper, which allows the dishwasher to be set back inside and closed off with doors. (The hardware used for entertainment centers, which allows the doors to open and slide back into a recess, would add to the convenience. Naturally a somewhat wider opening would be required.) Regular cabinet doors would also work (or even a curtain).

Another problem often encountered when trying to fit a dishwasher into an existing old kitchen is that modern dishwashers are all 24 inches deep, whereas old counters often measure only 18 or 20 inches deep. Some European dishwashers (Bosch, Miele, Asko) are slightly shallower, about 23 inches. A countertop dishwasher from Equator Appliance, measuring about 20 inches square, is one solution. It can be hooked up to the sink as a portable or installed permanently in a cabinet. Another option is to let the dishwasher stick out and build a wooden frame around the part that protrudes. If the countertop is being replaced, it can step out over the protruding dishwasher, which will make the whole thing look intentional. A third option is recessing it into the wall, which will gain a couple of inches. Sometimes there isn't room for a full 24-inch-wide standard dishwasher, in which case an 18-inch-wide model (offered by several manufacturers) may solve the problem. Unfortunately, an 18-inch-wide model costs the same as a big one. Another problem with installing a dishwasher in an existing kitchen is locating the air gap. (This is the silver cylinder required by code and usually made of plastic.) Modern sinks with deck-mounted faucets have an extra hole for the air gap, but an old sink with wall-mounted faucets does not. With a tile-in sink it will be necessary to cut a hole in the counter for the air gap. Try using a carbide hole saw made for cutting tile. If the counter is being newly tiled, make the hole first and cut the tile to fit around it. If you have a big porcelain sink with drain boards, it's unlikely the dishwasher will fit underneath it anyway, so it will have to be located elsewhere.

A MICROWAVE HIDES IN A CABINET WITH A TILT-UP DOOR, AND A PULL-OUT CUTTING BOARD BELOW PROVIDES A PLACE TO SET THE FOOD AFTER HEATING. THE DOOR USES A FLUSH-MOUNTED RING PULL, OFTEN FOUND ON BOATS.

FAST FOOD

Obviously there were no microwaves in the Arts & Crafts period. In fact, the first microwave oven was manufactured by Amana in 1947: it weighed seven hundred and fifty pounds and stood five feet tall. Needless to say, microwaves were only used commercially until 1967, when the first countertop model for the home was introduced. Like any new technology, there was initial resistance because people were unsure how to cook with them, just as there had been resistance when stoves were introduced because people were used to cooking in fireplaces. Today, even a five-year-old knows how to make microwave popcorn, and, frankly, even if its only function was to reheat coffee, a microwave would still be a useful appliance.

Obsessive Restoration

If you're determined to have a completely period kitchen, I guess there's always reheating coffee on the stove . . .

Compromise Solution

Fortunately, it's very easy to hide a microwave: in an upper cabinet; in a small cabinet suspended from an upper cabinet, perhaps with a drop-down door; in a lower cabinet; or in a countertop appliance garage (with real cabinet doors—not tambour doors); or possibly just out on the counter, although some larger models may not fit underneath existing upper cabinets, which were often hung lower than present-day cabinets. Mounting a microwave above the stove is a bit obvious; a less-obtrusive method is better.

A Detroit Jewel "They Bake Better" stove sets the color scheme for this kitchen. On the marble-topped island, ingredients for baking are assembled. A high subway-tile wainscot implies that the original owner was wealthy enough to afford this luxury. Reproduction pendant light fixtures are simple and understated. On the left, a breakfast room with French doors to the garden is a step down from the kitchen.

Douglas fir panels that match the cabinets completely cover this modern bottom-mount refrigerator. The compressor panel is covered with a louvered wooden panel. Unlike this one, most refrigerators that accept panels leave the obviously modern aluminum edge showing. Brass handles have been added.

SQUASH, ANYONE?

Other than questioning why you need one, the same rules and solutions apply to trash compactors as to dishwashers. If possible, put them out on the utility porch or in the pantry.

THE DAILY GRIND

The first garbage disposal was introduced by the In-Sink-Erator Company in 1938. It eliminated one of the most disgusting kitchen tasks: emptying the slimy residue out of the sink strainer. Actually, really old sinks didn't have removable strainers, which made it even worse. Some articles in period magazines make mention of having to remove the sink trap occasionally to empty out the accumulated grease and other substances. Disposals can't be retrofitted to many old sinks because the drain hole is too small, about the size of a bathroom sink drain, but newer sinks with larger drains are candidates for a disposal. It isn't even necessary to grind very much waste in them; it's just for the random stuff that's rinsed off the plates.

TOAST OF THE TOWN

With the advent of reliable electric power, manufacturers fell all over themselves introducing such labor-saving electric appliances as irons (1903), percolators (1908), toasters (1910), waffle irons (1918), vacuum cleaners (1924), and mixers. Many of these are still available through antiques dealers and shops and may still be functional. Modern small appliances, such as bread makers, toaster ovens, and food processors, can be easily hidden in cabinets.

THE ICEBOX OF THE 1911 LANTERMAN HOUSE IS FACED WITH WHITE SUBWAY TILE.

CHAMBERS STOVES ARE HIGHLY COLLECTIBLE AND BEAUTIFULLY DESIGNED. A FOLD-DOWN PORCELAIN TOP COVERS THE BURNERS WHEN NOT IN USE. IN THE RIGHT REAR IS A DEEP WELL BURNER. THE STOVE VENTS DIRECTLY OUT THE BACK THROUGH THE WALL.

THE GENERAL ELECTRIC MONITOR TOP WAS SO POPULAR IT SOON GAVE RISE TO ASSOCIATED TRINKETS LIKE THIS CLOCK AND SALT AND PEPPER SHAKERS, SHOWN ON TOP. THE CABINETS WERE ALL BUILT BY THE HOMEOWNER, USING (APPROPRIATELY) A CRAFTSMAN-BRAND TABLE SAW FROM SEARS.

A TINY ICEBOX GRACES THIS BUT-LER'S PANTRY. PERHAPS IT WAS USED TO KEEP A FROZEN DESSERT FROM MELTING TILL IT WAS SERVED.

LEFT: A BUILT-IN ICEBOX AT THE 1905 ROBINSON HOUSE BY GREENE & GREENE IS FRAMED WITH WOOD. THIS PART OF THE HOUSE HAD NOT YET BEEN RESTORED WHEN THE PHOTO WAS TAKEN. ■■ RIGHT: LARGE LOWER CABINETS WITH GREENE & GREENE–STYLE WOODEN DOORS COPIED FROM THE ONES IN THE MAIN HOUSE HIDE UNDER-THE-COUNTER REFRIGERATORS IN A NEW KITCHEN BUILT IN THE CARRIAGE HOUSE AT THE ROBINSON HOUSE.

I N THE BUTLER'S PANTRY OF THE DUNSMUIR HOUSE, THE ORIGINAL ICEBOX, SHEATHED IN WHITE GLASS AND NICKEL-PLATED STRAPS, SITS BENEATH A TRAY STORAGE CABINET. THE AMUSING LITTLE LONG-LEGGED CABINET MAY BE A LATER ADDITION.

A 1919 MODEL QUICK MEAL STOVE HAS SIX BURNERS, TWO OVENS, A BROILER, AND A WARMING OVEN. THE GAS PIPING BENEATH THE BURNERS IS EXPOSED. ■■ OPPOSITE: A MAGIC CHEF STOVE WITH A FOLD-DOWN TOP THAT COVERS THE BURNERS HAS A SLEEK LOOK. THE OVEN CONTROL IS ON THE RIGHT SIDE.

L ARGE CERAMIC HEXAGONAL TILES MAKE UP THE FLOOR IN THE KITCHEN OF THE 1911 LANTERMAN HOUSE IN LA CAÑADA–FLINTRIDGE, CALIFORNIA. THE 1940S-
ERA STOVE REPLACED AN EARLIER MODEL.

E VEN A 1960S-ERA STOVE CAN LOOK RIGHT IN AN OLD KITCHEN. THIS ONE
IS ACCOMPANIED BY A NEW MARBLE-TOPPED CABINET, WHICH PROVIDES A
BIT OF COUNTER SPACE.

Layout and Design

If you are restoring an original kitchen and don't plan to change anything, then layout will not be a concern. However, if you are starting from scratch or trying to adapt an original kitchen to allow for modern appliances, then layout will become an issue. The basic layout concepts have not changed much since the 1920s and 1930s. The concept of the work triangle is that the distance between the three

A WALL, WHICH RAN FROM THE MIDDLE OF WHERE THE DISHWASHER CURRENTLY RESIDES AND ENDED WHERE THE RIGHT HAND LIGHT FIXTURE IS LOCATED, DIVIDED THIS KITCHEN INTO TWO CLAUSTROPHOBIC ROOMS, A 5-FOOT-WIDE KITCHEN AND A 6 x 6-FOOT BREAKFAST ROOM. THE KITCHEN SIDE WAS CRAMPED FURTHER BY A COOLER CABINET, WHICH SAT TO THE LEFT OF THE SINK AND CAME ALL THE WAY DOWN TO THE COUNTER. REMOVING THE WALL OPENED UP THE KITCHEN, ALLOWING MORE LIGHT FROM THE LARGER WINDOWS IN THE BREAKFAST ROOM. ORIGINAL CABINETS ON THE RIGHT WERE ENHANCED WITH A RUN OF NEW CABINETS ALONG THE SINK WALL, AS WELL AS NEW CABINETS ON THE STOVE SIDE (NOT SHOWN). THERE IS STILL ROOM FOR AN EATING AREA.

main kitchen elements (sink, stove, and refrigerator) should be no less than 4 feet and no more than 9 feet, and that the total measurement of the three sides should not exceed 26 feet for maximum efficiency. This concept led to the most common kitchen layouts still in use: the U shape, the L shape, the galley (everything on two opposing walls), the Pullman (everything on one wall, usually found in apartments), and the island (usually combined with the L or U shape). Variations on these basic layouts abound, and new kitchens may contain angled peninsulas, trapezoidal or free-form islands, or curved counters. Most of these would not be appropriate in a period kitchen. A layout that keeps traffic out of the work areas (so you are not tripping over guests, kids, or dogs) is something to aim for, although in an old kitchen it may not always be possible. Present-day kitchens may also contain additional work areas beyond the basic three, including baking centers, snack centers, computer centers, secondary sinks, and such. If you are starting from scratch and have the room, you may be able to fit in some of these.

ARCHAEOLOGY

The existing kitchen may be completely original, though this is rare. Often some parts of it may have been altered while others have been left alone. Figuring out which parts have been altered is not always possible, but there are clues. Sometimes cabinets have been removed but often find a new home in the basement, garage, or attic. Frequently some cabinets, but not all of them, are replaced with new ones.

One of the most common alterations is countertop replacement where original wood or tile counters have been replaced with different tile or laminate. Sometimes the old counter is still underneath. Sinks often get replaced. Possibly a wall-hung sink or a sink on legs was replaced with a tile-in sink at a later date, or a sink that got chipped was replaced with a newer model.

Another common alteration is the replacement of original cabinet doors with newer slab doors. Look for "ghosts" of old hinges or old mortises along the face frame, and look inside for evidence that cabinets were built in place (plaster as the back wall) or have bead-board backs (later cabi-

IF THE EXISTING COUNTER ISN'T DEEP ENOUGH FOR A DISHWASHER, THERE IS ALWAYS THE OPTION OF ALLOWING IT TO STICK OUT AND BUILDING A BOX AROUND IT AS THESE HOMEOWNERS HAVE. IF NEW COUNTERTOPS ARE BEING INSTALLED, BUMPING THEM OUT OVER THE DISHWASHER WILL MAKE IT LOOK AS IF IT WAS DONE ON PURPOSE.

nets had plywood or hardboard backs). Cooler cabinets often are removed or the vents are boarded up (look for vents on the outside of the wall, or holes in the floor). Hardware and light fixtures were often changed. Cracked plaster ceilings may be hiding above suspended ceilings or glued-on acoustic tiles, and, of course, floor coverings have usually been replaced.

USING WHAT YOU HAVE

If the existing kitchen is completely original and you want to keep it, perhaps only cosmetic work will be required: repainting or refinishing the cabinets, replacing worn flooring, regrouting the tile, and so forth. If you don't mind the refrigerator being on the back porch or the water heater being next to the stove, no problem. But if

you want to incorporate some modern technology like a dishwasher or new refrigerator, then some adaptation will have to take place.

The two most difficult things to incorporate are a modern refrigerator and a dishwasher. Finding space for a refrigerator in a kitchen where it originally resided on the back porch can be difficult. They are pretty large and bulky (averaging 32 inches wide, 30 inches deep, and 60 inches high), and it's best to have them at the end of a run of cabinets, if possible. Built-in refrigerators are less deep (24 inches) but usually wider, not to mention more expensive. Refrigerator and freezer drawers (also expensive) are an option that allows splitting up the functions into different areas. It may be possible to recess the refrigerator into the wall somewhere by bumping out into unused space in a closet, another room, over a stairway, or even the outside wall of the house. A lot of times the only place there is room for it is right next to the stove; this is not the best place but may be the only choice.

A dishwasher is also difficult to incorporate if the existing cabinets are less than 24 inches deep, as they often are. Finding a place to put it is easy enough; usually a cabinet, bin, or bank of drawers can be sacrificed to make room for it. I recommend the following options: recessing it into the wall behind the cabinets, which may gain enough inches for it to fit flush; letting it stick out and building a wooden frame around that part (possibly incorporating it into an island); or consider purchasing a European dishwasher brand that is shallower than 24 inches. Occasionally the layout is such that the sink cabinet and an adjacent cabinet can be replaced with deeper cabinets to allow for a dishwasher, especially if the sink is on the short end of an ell.

Because hot water in early kitchens was heated by the stove, you may still have a water heater in your kitchen.

Sometimes they were in a closet, which is not a problem unless that closet space would be more useful for something else. Often they were out in the open, and unless you have a lovely old one that still functions, you might want to figure out a way to get the water heater out of the kitchen. It can be moved to the basement, utility porch, or a closet, although this may involve running a new flue as well. There are also code requirements about the amount of air available for combustion, which may dictate where you can put it. Another option is the "instant" water heater (such as the Aquastar), which is far more energy efficient and takes up much less room, although it may not be allowed by local code.

FINDING SPACE

Because we have more things in our kitchens than they did in the early twentieth century, an old kitchen may or may not have sufficient cabinet or counter space. If it doesn't, there may be areas where more cabinets can be added. It may be that the only counter or cabinet space is on either side of the sink and that other walls may be candidates for adding some. An old stove frequently stood by itself and was quite large (up to 60 inches wide). If you have a smaller stove, there may be an opportunity to add cabinets around it. Stoves were located in front of or next to a chimney, so if the stove no longer needs to be vented, and the labor of doing so would be worthwhile, removing the chimney (assuming it doesn't also serve the furnace or some other heat source) may gain some space that could be put to use. Sometimes removing a built-in ironing board, an unused dumbwaiter, or a clothes chute will provide some usable space (such as for a spice cabinet). Perhaps the addition of a worktable (which

A PULL-OUT TABLE CAN PROVIDE EXTRA WORKSPACE WITHOUT TAKING UP VALUABLE FLOOR SPACE. ALTHOUGH THIS TABLE IS NEW, PULL-OUT OR FOLD-DOWN TABLES ARE IN THE FINE TRADITION OF SPACE-SAVING BUNGALOW BUILT-INS. THIS PARTICULAR TABLE SITS UNDERNEATH AN UNOBTRUSIVE FLAT GLASS COOKTOP SET INTO THE GRANITE COUNTER. A BREAKFAST NOOK IS TUCKED INTO A CORNER NEXT TO THE SINK.

THE REFRIGERATOR WAS ORIGI-
NALLY LOCATED WHERE THE
STOOL SITS IN THIS PICTURE, WHICH
WAS ABOUT SIXTEEN FEET AWAY
FROM THE STOVE AND THE SINK. IT
WAS MOVED CLOSER AND A WALL
BUILT BEHIND IT, MAKING FOR A
MORE EFFICIENT LAYOUT. THE FAR
END OF THE KITCHEN ESSENTIALLY
BECAME A PANTRY. TO THE RIGHT OF
THE STOOL, ONE DOOR LEADS TO
THE BREAKFAST ROOM, WHILE ON
THE LEFT, ANOTHER DOOR LEADS TO
THE BACK HALL. BEHIND THE
REFRIGERATOR WALL, ANOTHER
DOOR OPENS TO THE HALLWAY. A
CABINET WAS ADDED NEXT TO THE
REFRIGERATOR PROVIDING COUNTER
SPACE FOR UNLOADING GROCERIES.

many of these kitchens were meant to have) or an island will help, bearing in mind that islands during the period were basically glorified worktables and did not contain sinks or cooktops as modern ones often do. If your house still has a pantry or a butler's pantry, space may be available there. It is interesting that new houses are starting to have pantries again, an indication that we have returned to the bulk buying of our ancestors, only now it's done at warehouse clubs.

Slightly more drastic methods for finding space include removing walls (think long and hard about this, and don't do it just because your architect or designer tells you to). On the other hand, sometimes a wall is just plain stupid, such as one dividing a 10 x 12-foot room into a tiny breakfast room and an even tinier kitchen. Sometimes walling up a relatively useless door will make a difference, and, often, shortening a window with a low sill or even removing a window altogether may allow more counter space. Again, don't do this just for the heck of it. It's expensive to move plumbing work, so leave the sink where it is.

These days we expect to have eating space in the kitchen, and, unless the original kitchen had a breakfast nook, it may be difficult to find space for it. It may be possible to convert a utility porch over to that use or to use a worktable for that purpose. A fold-down table may serve, and that was a common solution at the time. There *were*

no breakfast bars. All the spaces in these houses were meant to be used, unlike today's houses with their vestigial living and dining rooms, so here's a radical idea: eat all your meals in the dining room.

A more difficult thing to accommodate is today's expectation that the kitchen open to the outdoors, to a deck or porch. Although there was much talk during the Arts & Crafts period about opening the house to the outdoors, they were talking primarily about the *front* of the house. The kitchen and the back of the house were considered utility areas. The route to the backyard usually went through the utility room or laundry; on occasion, the back door itself might have been a French door, but it was usually single. A breakfast room might have had double French doors leading to a porch or side yard, but there is very little precedent for today's double French doors with sidelights and transoms. Going that route will forever brand the kitchen as belonging to the turn of the twenty-first century. A single French door or a very basic set of double doors might be an acceptable compromise.

OLD AND NEW

Adding new cabinets, windows, and such to existing old parts of the kitchen requires matching door and drawer styles, old moldings, hardware, and so forth. A new or shortened window should match an existing old one. If the old windows are gone, rip out those aluminum sliders and replace them all with real wooden windows. Matching old moldings may mean having new ones custom-made.

AN ISLAND, A POT RACK, AND OTHER CUSTOMIZED STORAGE WERE ADDED TO THE KITCHEN OF THIS PLAN-BOOK BUNGALOW. TO THE LEFT OF THE STOVE IS A PULLOUT PANTRY AS WELL AS A NARROW SLOT FOR TRAYS. THE FAR SIDE OF THE ISLAND CONTAINS A WINE RACK.

IF YOU JUST HAVE TO HAVE A BREAKFAST BAR, IT SHOULD LOOK LIKE THIS. THE TILED COUNTERTOP ECHOES THE TILE ON THE SINK SIDE OF THE ROOM. A FUNC-
TIONING CRANK PHONE AND VINTAGE FAN ADD TO THE PERIOD LOOK, ALTHOUGH BEHIND THE LACE CURTAIN LURKS A SMALL TELEVISION SET. TO THE RIGHT OF THE
STOVE IS A CLOSET THAT ONCE HELD THE WATER HEATER. AN OLD ELECTRIC STOVE ADDS TO THE AMBIENCE.

STARTING FROM SCRATCH

Perhaps you have a kitchen so dreadful that all you can do is rip it out and start over. While this may not be the cheapest alternative, in many ways it is much easier. Constraints such as doorways, windows, chimneys, and the like will remain and will have to be worked around. But starting with a clean slate will allow for much more customization of storage and prep areas than might otherwise be possible and provide a kitchen that looks original but is more functional in modern terms. It may not have all the bells and whistles currently available, but in 1916 it would have been unbelievably hip and trendy. If starting from scratch, take some time to analyze how you cook and what kinds of things need to be stored. A pantry is useful if the space is available for it.

Assessing Your Needs and Dealing with Professsionals

The first thing to do when renovating your kitchen is to look inside—not inside the kitchen, inside yourself. A lot of questions need to be answered before you ever hire a contractor or purchase an appliance. Answer the questions honestly—the test will not be graded. Do you cook? A lot, or hardly ever? If the answer is hardly ever, perhaps you don't need that six-burner restaurant stove. Are you a slob? Then perhaps a marbleized linoleum

A TYPICAL KITCHEN BEFORE DEMOLITION. IN THIS PARTICULAR KITCHEN, THE SINK WAS DAMAGED, THE FAUCET LEAKED, THE GROUT HAD DETERIORATED, ALLOWING WATER TO GET UNDER THE TILE AND ROT THE WOOD, THE GLASS CABINET KNOBS HAD BEEN REPLACED, AND A LARGE PLASTER STOVE HOOD COMPLETELY DOMINATED THE ROOM. A LINOLEUM COUNTER (AT RIGHT) WAS ALSO DAMAGED. AND THE WHOLE THING HAD SEVENTY-ODD YEARS OF GREASE AND NICOTINE ON IT.

SAME KITCHEN, DEMOLITION IN PROCESS. IT'S NOT JUST THE DEMOLITION THAT GENERATES DIRT. OFTEN AN ORIGINAL KITCHEN WILL BE ABSOLUTELY FILTHY, AND SOME PEOPLE DEAL WITH THAT BETTER THAN OTHERS. TRY TO LOOK BEYOND THE DIRT (SEE THIS KITCHEN FINISHED ON PAGE 117). A LARGE POWERFUL SHOP-VACUUM IS AN ABSOLUTE NECESSITY. BUY A REPLACEMENT GORE-TEX FILTER FOR IT; THE PAPER FILTERS DON'T FILTER PLASTER DUST VERY WELL.

floor is a better choice than a black-and-white checkerboard. Do you have kids? Try using something other than glass knobs on the cabinets. Do you entertain a lot? Do you want to eat in the kitchen? Do you like lots of stuff on the counters, or do you like everything behind closed doors? If you have glass doors, will you arrange everything neatly? Will that be a hassle? Or do you not care if it's messy? Do you want a pantry? Do you buy things in bulk? If you have brass hardware, will you care if it tarnishes? If it does tarnish, will you polish it?

Do you want to do all or some of it yourself? Do you have the skills, or do you think you can learn them? Do you have the time? (It will likely take longer than estimated.) Do you know which things to leave to professionals? Do you want to act as your own general contractor? Would you rather just hire someone to do all of it and vacation in Europe till it's finished? Can you afford to stay in Europe that long? What is your budget? What happens if you go beyond it (and you will)? Are you decisive or do you change your mind every five minutes? If you have other people in the house, they must also answer these questions.

DECISIONS, DETRITUS, DUST, AND DISTRESS

Most people are not prepared for the stress of renovation. They are surprised to find themselves upset by the demolition process, which leaves a gaping wound in a previously intact house. No matter how bad the old kitchen was, you may still find the renovation disturbing. There are seemingly endless decisions to be made, even for a period kitchen, and eventually you will find yourself in the middle of a heated argument about hardware with either the contractor or your significant other or both. After a few months, the novelty of having the refrigerator in the dining room and eating nothing but frozen dinners and take-out will have worn off, and you will be really cranky. You will be even crankier if you have been doing the dishes in the bathroom sink all that time. Everything you own will be covered with plaster dust, no matter how much effort is made to keep it out of the rest of the house, and you will begin to question your own sanity. The one valuable thing you forgot to put away for safekeeping will get broken. You will begin to fantasize about moving into a brand new condominium and giving up this old-house stuff altogether.

There is a particular form of stress attached to restoring or redoing a period kitchen, and that is overcoming the objections of all the people you will be dealing with in order to get what you want. You will constantly hear the following phrases: "Nobody makes those anymore." "You can't do it that way." "Why would you want that?" "Nobody uses _____ anymore." "Why don't you tear out all this plaster and put up drywall?" "You need to get rid of some of these doors and open up the space." "Think what you're doing to the resale value."

Then there is your family. Even if you and your significant other are in agreement, it is entirely possible that your children, your parents, your siblings, your real-estate agent, and/or your neighbors will believe you have completely lost your mind. As things start to go wrong or the project starts to go over budget, they will become more vocal and you will begin to wonder if perhaps they are right. Try to ignore them and remember that you are doing the right thing for your house and for future generations. None of the naysayers will buy this argument, but they don't have to; only you do.

Hopefully, this book will give you the ammunition needed to stand firm in the face of these objections in order to get the kitchen you have in mind.

CREWS CONTROL

Even if you are doing the entire renovation yourself, there are still many people to deal with. You may not be dealing with every one of these people, but you'll definitely be dealing with some of them. Try to keep in mind at all times that they are working for *you*, since they will sometimes lose sight of that fact. Also bear in mind that many of them have their own agendas, often involving parting you from large amounts of your money (not that they are necessarily dishonest, merely less than objective). It's important to educate yourself so you know where it is appropriate to spend a lot of money and where it isn't.

THE ARCHITECT MAY NOT BE WRONG IN WANTING TO "OPEN UP THE SPACE." CERTAINLY IT WAS AN IMPROVEMENT IN THIS KITCHEN, WHICH WAS TRANSFORMED FROM TWO TINY CRAMPED ROOMS INTO A LARGER 12 x 12-FOOT ROOM. WHILE THAT IS FAR FROM HUGE, THE ADDED LIGHT FROM THE WINDOWS IN THE BREAKFAST ROOM AND THE VIEW INTO THE BACKYARD GIVE A SENSE OF MORE SPACE.

Even if you have a lot of money, there is no need to spend it foolishly. There are good, bad, and mediocre people in every field, so be sure to get references and referrals and check them out. Also realize that there are very few people who understand period kitchens, so it may be more difficult to find the right people for your project.

ARCHITECTS

Unless you are planning an addition or some really major structural changes, you probably don't need an architect. An architect will tell you otherwise, of course, right after commenting that you "need to replace this door with an arch in order to open up the space." They may also want to be creative and express themselves, usually at the expense of the building.

PARTWAY THROUGH THE REMODEL, THINGS ARE STARTING TO LOOK A LITTLE MORE CIVILIZED. ONCE THERE IS PLYWOOD ON TOP OF THE CABINETS AND THE SINK IS HOOKED UP, IT'S ALMOST LIKE A REAL KITCHEN AGAIN, THOUGH THERE IS STILL MUCH TO BE DONE.

If you are doing something major, I would certainly interview a lot of architects. Ask to see pictures of other kitchens they've done. Assess whether they will be receptive to your wants and needs. If you feel you are being talked down to or if they seem like they have an agenda, keep looking.

There are architects who specialize in historic preservation projects, though this won't necessarily mean they know anything about period kitchens. You can hire an architect to oversee the whole project, or you can hire one just for the design and drawings. You can even hire one by the hour for feedback. Sometimes an architect can be useful for coming up with a creative solution to a difficult layout problem. Using one will usually add to the cost of the project, though occasionally it can actually save you money.

CONTRACTORS AND SUBCONTRACTORS

Unless you plan to do every single thing yourself, you will probably be hiring contractors. You can hire a general contractor to take charge of the entire project, who will hire subcontractors (plumbers, electricians, tile setters, etc.) as needed for various specialty jobs. A general contractor will put a mark-up on the work of the subs (if the plumber charges $800 for the plumbing, the contractor will bill you $1,000), so you can save money by acting as the general contractor and hiring subs directly. However, this means you need to have the time and also some knowledge of the order in which things need to be done so as to schedule the subs. It can be hard to get cooperation from the subs, who tend to be loyal to the contractors who give them steady work, making you last on the list. You also need to have the time to be on the job site to make sure things are going as planned, so it's not a good idea for someone with a full-time job to be their own general contractor. If you're hiring one, all the usual caveats apply: get references, get at least three bids, make sure all the bids are for the same scope of work, have a written contract, and so forth. I would recommend getting a few books on the subject from your library or bookstore, or peruse one of the many articles on this subject to be found in various shelter magazines.

But here are a few other words of wisdom based on my experience. If you're dealing with a contracting firm (as opposed to a one- or two-person business), bear in mind that the person they send to talk to you and present the bid is basically a salesperson who may be extremely personable and will assure you that of course it can all be done on schedule and on budget. But this is not who you will be dealing with on a day-to-day basis. Ask to meet the foreman and the crew who will be working on your project. Go to a job site where that person is working now and observe the crew. You will be involved in a fairly intimate relationship with these people, so it will be much less stressful if you actually like them. Talk to the person who will be in charge of your project. Is that person respectful or are you hearing some of the phrases detailed earlier in this chapter? Is that person receptive to old homes or is there an underlying attitude that newer is always better, or that existing things are not worth saving. This attitude will play out in various ways: wanting to replace all the plaster with drywall instead of patching it, wanting to replace the existing windows instead of fixing them, wanting to rip out perfectly functional original cabinets because they are a little banged up, insisting that *all* the plumbing in the house must be replaced with copper, and so forth. My philosophy can be summed up in a different phrase: "If it ain't broke, don't fix it." Go with your gut instinct, because if you don't get along with them now, things will not improve later.

Knowledge is power. The best thing to do is to educate yourself as much as possible about the construction process. You don't need to be able to *do* everything, but it helps to understand the various ways it *could* be done. It helps to know the jargon as well. And remember, their primary motivation is money. Once you make that final payment, they're gone, whether they're actually finished or not.

ELECTRICIANS

The good thing about electricians is that they tend to be a little more focused than most subs because they realize that electricity can kill you if you don't pay attention. They seem to fall into two categories: those who are willing to "fish" wires through small holes (which is tedious and time-consuming) and those who prefer to open up the entire stud bay and let someone else patch the plaster later. You can save a lot of money by "fishing" the wires yourself and having the electrician make the final connections. Try to find someone who has experience in old houses who will be able to deal with the existing knob-and-tube wiring. It is not necessary to rip it all out if it is still in good condition.

PLUMBERS

Try to find someone who has experience with old plumbing, who might be willing to rebuild your old faucet instead of trying to convince you to buy a new one, and who will not be completely aghast at the idea that you might actually *want* separate hot and cold taps.

CABINETMAKERS

A period kitchen is likely to involve custom cabinets. All the kitchen magazines will tell you this is the most expensive option, and it can be, especially if you go crazy with custom finishes or really expensive hardware. But for the simple cabinets that are appropriate to a period kitchen, it is actually a less-expensive alternative.

Here is the magic question to ask of potential cabinetmakers: "Can you make flush inset doors?" If the reply is some variation on "nobody makes those anymore," then keep looking. If the answer is yes, proceed to ask about cabinets without toe-kicks, mortised hinges, and wooden drawer runners. If the answer is still yes, you may have found the person you are looking for. I have had good luck using those who just build cabinets, and not those who prefer to be building elaborate furniture with inlays of rare South American hardwoods; they may be bored building your plain Shaker-door cabinets.

There are also large custom cabinet companies that ship nationwide. These are available directly to consumers or through kitchen showrooms and designers.

CARPENTERS

If you are doing a lot of the work yourself, you might

only need to hire a carpenter for the more complex framing or finish work (installing windows, hanging the cabinets, installing trim and molding). Finish carpentry has a different skill set than framing, and not all carpenters will be good at both. Unpainted woodwork and cabinets require a higher level of finish carpentry because mistakes can't be rectified with filler and paint.

PAINTERS

The main thing to remember about painters is that they will paint anything that has not been removed or masked off, so take off or mask all the hardware, switch plates, light fixtures, and anything else you don't want painted. Don't wait for them to do it. If they are spraying, you might want to remove furniture, rugs, and such from adjacent rooms. Some are neater than others.

TILE SETTERS

Setting tile is pretty messy, and a good tile setter will mask off the cabinets and anything else in order to keep off mortar and grout. If you are doing very simple tile, you won't necessarily need a high-end installer who specializes in really elaborate installations. Tile stores are usually a good source of referrals.

FLOORING INSTALLERS

Usually the flooring store has installers who they contract with or employ. As noted in the flooring chapter, installing linoleum is different from installing vinyl, so make sure the person they send has experience with linoleum, especially if any inlay is involved.

KITCHEN AND INTERIOR DESIGNERS

If you are not confident about designing your own kitchen, you may want to employ an interior designer. She

or he can help with layout and choosing various kitchen elements as well as decor. However, as with other professionals, designers may have little understanding of period kitchens and may suggest things that are currently stylish but inappropriate to an old kitchen. Kitchen designers deal specifically with kitchens and are often found at kitchen/bath showrooms, cabinet companies, home centers, and design/building contractors. They have more training and education in the specifics of kitchens. Be aware that those employed by showrooms will naturally want to sell you the products carried by that showroom. Like interior designers, they may know little about period kitchens, but they can be helpful in solving layout and other problems.

BUILDING INSPECTORS

If you are redoing your kitchen with permits, you (or your contractor) will be dealing with the building department and whatever version of the building code has been adopted in your area, with a few state and local regulations thrown in for good measure. The building code is concerned with health and safety issues. A little-known fact is that the building code is driven by insurance companies, who look at accident statistics having to do with buildings and try to figure out ways to prevent those accidents through different building practices.

The chances of such things happening are statistically quite small, yet the code is continually changed in an attempt to prevent them. It is aimed primarily at new construction, and thus causes many problems for historic buildings. There are many things in historic buildings that met code when they were built but do not meet today's code. Sometimes there have been improvements in technology that make sense to incorporate (grounded outlets, for instance), but other things do not (like mandating fluorescent lights to save energy, when far more energy could be saved by mandating insulation retrofits). Trying to make an old house comply with modern code can be difficult, and whatever latitude you may get to do it in ways that do not impact the historic look will be entirely at the whim of your local building inspector.

AKE SURE A WALL ISN'T LOAD-BEARING BEFORE REMOVING IT. IF THE FLOOR JOISTS OR CEILING JOISTS RUN PARALLEL TO THE WALL, IT'S USUALLY NOT LOAD-BEARING (BUT CHECK WITH AN EXPERT). A LOAD-BEARING WALL CAN BE REMOVED BUT WILL NEED A BEAM IN ITS PLACE TO CARRY THE LOAD. ELECTRICAL WIRING WILL COMPLICATE WALL REMOVAL. TAKING OUT THIS WALL MADE THIS KITCHEN BRIGHTER AND LESS CLAUSTROPHOBIC.

Some states have adopted a Historic Building Code or something like it. This is a code with more sensitivity to historic buildings. Unfortunately, to be eligible to use it, your house usually needs to be on some register: the National Register of Historic Places, the State Historic Register, or your local Historic Register. It is certainly worth looking into if your home qualifies. (Call your State Historic Preservation Office for information.)

Otherwise, it is entirely up to the local jurisdiction and the building inspector in particular whether you can hide your electrical outlets under the cabinets, install your antique gas/wood stove without a triple-wall flue, replace your windows with single-glazed panes that are historically correct, or have nothing but incandescent lights. Some cities and inspectors are remarkably flexible about this sort of thing, while others are infuriatingly obsessed with the letter rather than the spirit of the code. Some inspectors will go over the work of do-it-yourselfers with a particularly fine-tooth comb, while others will give a homeowner a lot more leeway. Some building departments will allow your contractor to get a permit using a pencil sketch of the project on the back of a napkin while requiring you as the homeowner to submit a full set of blueprints, and sometimes it's the other way around.

SALVAGE YARDS

If you want old stuff, eventually you'll end up at a salvage yard. There you will find much old stuff that is rusted, warped, or bent, at semi-outrageous prices. The stuff that is actually in decent condition will command even more outrageous prices. However, if you want a big sink with porcelain drain boards, a salvage yard is the best place to find one. Some things at a salvage yard will be cheaper than their new equivalents, and for the things that have no new equivalent, a salvage yard may be your only source. You will do much better on price by finding these things at estate sales or through private parties, but that isn't always possible. Salvage yards do provide a great service by recycling historic building parts that might otherwise go to the landfill.

HARDWARE STORES, HOME CENTERS, AND LUMBERYARDS

Old-fashioned hardware stores are indispensable. They will sell you the one washer you need to fix your faucet, may have all sorts of archaic hardware still in stock, and are rapidly becoming the last place to carry slotted screws.

They often employ people who have been around long enough to know something about old houses.

Home centers are certainly a fine place to buy joint compound, nails, plywood, thin-set mortar, basic tile, and such. The prices will be lower, and that may even balance out with the hassle of waiting in line. They sometimes even have a few suitable lighting fixtures, and often you can special-order something appropriate, be it a light fixture or a wooden screen door. Other than basic supplies, however, few of them carry much that would be appropriate or useful in a period kitchen.

A lumberyard is a must for real lumber, as home centers carry only the most basic sizes and woods. Real bead board, tongue-and-groove fir flooring, and 5/4 stock for cabinets will only be found at the lumberyard. Some yards also have milling capacity and can make trim and molding to match what is already in the house. There are also companies that specialize in moldings, flooring, or hardwoods, as well as companies that sell remilled wood salvaged from old buildings.

CATALOGS

Almost any kitchen element can probably be ordered through the mail or over the Internet: lighting, hardware, plumbing fixtures, cabinets, flooring, appliances, and so forth. This is especially useful to those living in areas where these kinds of items are not available.

DOING IT YOURSELF

If you have the time and the skills (or are willing to learn the skills), doing it yourself will give you the most control over the end result. It can save you a great deal of money, depending, of course, on how many tools you have to buy or rent and how many times you screw up. You may want to do only parts of it yourself and hire out the rest. Doing it yourself requires patience, at least some aptitude, and a willingness to leap into the unknown. And it helps if you like doing this kind of stuff.

Particular jobs that lend themselves to doing yourself are those that are not difficult but are tedious and time-consuming and, therefore, expensive to pay others to do. These include cleaning, paint- and wallpaper-stripping, stripping paint from hardware, polishing hardware, and picking up needed supplies. (Why pay your contractor to stand in line at the home center?) Other fairly easy tasks include paint prep, painting, patching small holes in plaster, and installing hardware, shelf coverings, and curtain rods. For those with more do-it-yourself experience, tasks such as installing ceramic tile, repairing wooden windows, laying vinyl tile, installing light fixtures or faucets, and even hanging and taping drywall would be possible. Tasks

Particular jobs that lend themselves to doing yourself are those that are not difficult but are tedious and time-consuming and, therefore, expensive to pay others to do.

for the really advanced might include running new wiring or plumbing, building an addition, laying sheet flooring, building cabinets, or plastering. Many how-to books and magazines are available for all of these tasks.

It also helps to have the right tools. Some may be worth purchasing, depending on how much you are likely to use them. Some of the more expensive ones can be rented by the day or week. Beyond the usual hammer, screwdrivers, wrenches, and pliers that most home tool kits should have, here are a few tools that are indispensable for restoration: a flat pry bar, carbide paint scrapers, 5-in-1 tool, locking pliers, reciprocating saw, jigsaw, power miter saw, belt sander, random-orbit sander, table saw, power planer, circular saw, heat gun, and the biggest, most powerful shop vacuum you can afford. Other specialized woodworking tools are useful for building cabinets, and a wet saw is a must for cutting ceramic tile. This is not an exhaustive list by any means, and tools needed will depend on what you're going to be doing.

There is also the issue of time versus money. Doing it yourself will probably take longer. You may be better off spending that time at work earning the money to pay a contractor. Do you really want to spend all your evenings and weekends working on the kitchen?

THIS PRAIRIE-STYLE BUNGALOW KITCHEN REPLACED A DREADFUL 1980S REMODEL. USING THE ORIGINAL PLANS AND ELEVATIONS, WHICH HAD BEEN PUBLISHED IN *THE BUNGALOW* MAGAZINE, THE KITCHEN WAS RETURNED TO ITS 1916 LOOK. ALTHOUGH THE GLASS-DOOR CABINETS WERE ORIGINALLY PLAIN, THE ARCHITECT CHOSE TO ADD THE MUNTIN PATTERNS THAT MATCH THE OTHER WINDOWS IN THE HOUSE. THESE CABINETS HAVE OVERLAY DOORS, WHICH SIT ON TOP OF THE FACE FRAME, RATHER THAN THE MORE COMMON INSET DOORS.

Resources

The main point of this book was to gather a great deal of information about period kitchens in one place, so that it would not be necessary for everyone who was re-doing a kitchen to reinvent the wheel. To that end I have tried to make this list as complete as possible, but I can hardly cover every single town in the country. There may be local sources available for many products needed in a kitchen restoration, and I would urge you to deal locally wherever possible. I have included some people and companies I have dealt with personally; this does not mean that other people or companies are not worthy of patronage, or that I have dealt with everyone on this list, or that I have managed to include everyone who ought to be included. Keep in mind also that not everything sold or made by the companies included in this resource list will be appropriate to a period kitchen.

APPLIANCES

VINTAGE

Apple Appliance
2973 Sacramento Street
Berkeley, CA 94702
(510) 841-8711

Barnstable Stove Shop
Box 472, Route 149
West Barnstable, MA 02668
(508) 362-9913

Brunelle Enterprises
203 Union Road
Wales, MA 01081
(413) 245-7396

**Erickson's Antiques
at The Depot**
Littleton, MA 01460
(508) 486-3589

Good Time Stove Co.
P.O. Box 306
Goshen, MA 01032
(413) 268-3677
(413) 268-9284 fax
www.goodtimestove.com

The Homestead
104 Railroad Avenue West
Skykomish, WA 98288
(360) 677-2840

Hugh's Place
6732 U.S. Hwy 190W
Port Allen, LA 70767
(225) 334-9118

**Johnny's Appliances and
Classic Ranges**
17549 Sonoma Highway
Sonoma, CA 95476
(707) 996-9730

Macy's Texas Stove Works
5515 Almeda Road
Houston, TX 77004
(713) 521-0934
(713) 521-0889 fax

Mill Creek Antiques
109 Newbury
Box 156
Paxico, KS 66526
(785) 636-5520

Pacific Stove Works
130 N. Salsipuedes Street, Ste. 3
Santa Barbara, CA 93103
(805) 962-0967

Old Appliance Club
P.O. Box 65
Ventura, CA 93002
(805) 643-3532
antiquestoves.com

J. Weaver All-Gas Appliances
4201 Market Street
Oakland, CA 94608
(510) 547-8766

NEW VINTAGE-STYLE APPLIANCES

Classic Cookers
90 Lower Barnett Hill
Middlesex, VT 05602
(802) 223-3620
(802) 223-7433 fax
(Aga cookstoves)

Elmira Stoveworks
595 Colby Drive
Waterloo, ON N2V 1A2
Canada
(519) 669-1281
(519) 725-5503 fax

Heartland Appliances
1050 Fountain Street North
Cambridge, ON N3H 4R7
Canada

House of Webster
P.O. Box 1988
1013 N. Second Street
Rogers, AR 72757
(501) 636-4640
(501) 636-2974 fax

Olde Stove Works
33507 Thompson Avenue
Mission, BC V2V 2W9
(604) 826-5669
(604) 826-9228 fax

NEW APPLIANCES

Amana
(800) 843-0304
www.amana.com

Asko
1161 Executive Drive West
Richardson, TX 75085
(800) 367-2444
(214) 644-8593 fax

Bosch Appliances
2800 S. 25th Avenue
Broadview, IL 60153
(800) 866-2022
www.boschappliances.com

Equator Corp.
10067 Timber Oak Drive
Houston, TX 77080
(800) 935-1955 x103
www.equatorappl.com
(countertop dishwashers)

Fisher and Paykel
22982 Alcalde Drive, Ste. 201
Laguna Hills, CA 92653
(888) 936-7872
(889) www.fisherpaykel.com
(dish drawers)

Frigidaire
104 Warren Road
Augusta, GA 30907
(800) 374-4432
www.frigidaire.com

General Electric Co.
Appliance Park
Bldg #3, Room 232
Louisville, KY 40225
(502) 452-4311
www.ge.com

KitchenAid
2302 Pipestone Road
Mail Drop #0120
Benton Harbor, MI 49022
(800) 422-1230
www.kitchenaid.com

Maytag Appliances
403 W. Fourth Street North
Newton, IA 50208
(877) 436-4642
www.maytag.com

Miele Appliances
9 Independence Way
Princeton, NJ 08540
(800) 843-7231
www.mieleusa.com

Sears Kenmore
(888) KENMORE
www.sears.com

U-Line Corp.
8900 N. 55th Street
Milwaukee, WI 53223
(414) 354-0300
(414) 354-7905 fax
www.u-line.com
(undercounter refrigerators)

Whirlpool
Benton Harbor, MI 49022
(800) 253-1301
www.whirlpool.com

CABINETRY

Steven Ballew
1521 - 37th Street
Sacramento, CA 95816
(916) 455-5908

Tim Brennan Co.,
Cabinetmakers
4 N. Oakwood Terrace
New Paltz, NY 12561
(914) 338-5757
(914) 338-5757 fax

Marion H. Campbell,
Cabinetmaker
39 Wall Street
Bethlehem, PA 18018
(610) 837-7775
(610) 837-7775 fax

Crown Point Cabinetry
153 Charlestown Road
Claremont, NH 03743
(800) 999-4994
(800) 370-1218 fax
www.crown-point.com

Crystal Cabinet Works
1100 Crystal Drive
Princeton. MN 55371
(800) 347-5045
(612) 389-3825 fax
www.ccworks.com

Decora
P.O. Box 420
One Aristokraft Square
Jasper, IN 47546
(812) 634-2288
www.decoracabinets.com

Bill Eichenberger
580 Irwin Street #6
San Rafael, CA 94901
(415) 457-1190

Heritage Custom Kitchens
215 Diller Avenue
New Holland, PA 17557
(717) 354-4011
(717) 355-0169 fax
www.hck.com

Hoosier Cabinet Co.
418 Wauregan Road
Brooklyn, CT 06234
(860) 774-7821
(restored and as-is Hoosier-style
kitchen cabinets)

Neil Kelly Cabinets
804 N. Alberta Street
Portland, OR 97217
(503) 335-9214
(503) 282-7932 fax
www.neilkelly.com

Kennebec Co.
1 Front Street
Bath, ME 04530
(207) 443-2131
(207) 443-4380 fax

Kraftmaid Cabinetry
(440) 632-5333
www.kraftmaid.com

Graham Lee Associates
2870 E. 54th Street
Vernon, CA 90058
(323) 581-8203
(323) 581-2536 fax
Brian Krueger

Michigan Hoosier Co.
1100 S. M-76
Sterling, MI 48659
(517) 654-9085
(517) 345-7098 fax
(Hoosier cabinet reproductions)

Christopher Peacock Cabinetry
151 Greenwich Avenue
Greenwich, CT 06830
(888) 609-9333
(203) 861-2762 fax

Plain and Fancy
Route 501 and Oak Street
Schaefferstown, PA 17088
(717) 949-6571
(717) 848-2114 fax

Plato Woodwork
200 Third Street SW
P.O. Box 98
Plato, MN 55370
(800) 328-5924
(320) 238-2131 fax

R and R Woodworks
P.O. Box 3084
Central Point, OR 97502
(541) 855-4428
(541) 855-8671 fax

Renaissance Cabinetmakers
RR 1 Box 2832
Arlington, VT 05250
(802) 375-9278
(802) 375-9278 fax

Restorations Unlimited
P.O. Box V
24 W. Main Street
Elizabethville, PA 17023
(717) 362-3477
(717) 362-4571 fax

Ring Leg Furnishings
Full Design Furniture, Bath
and Kitchen
134 Main Street
Gloucester, MA 01930
(978) 283-1039

Dana Robes, Wood Craftsman
Lower Shaker Village
P.O. Box 707
Enfield, NH 03748
(800) 722-5036
(603) 632-5377
www.danarobes.com

Rutt Custom Cabinetry
P.O. Box 129
1564 Main Street
Goodville, PA 17528
(717) 445-3700
www.rutt1.com

Strasser and Associates
35 Hillside Avenue
Monsey, NY 10952
(914) 425-0650
(914) 425-1842 fax

Wellborn Cabinet
38669 Hwy 77
P.O. Box 1210
Ashland, AL 36251
(800) 762-4475
(256) 354-7022 fax

Wood-Mode
#1 Second Street
Kreamer, PA 17833
(570) 374-2711
www.wood-mode.com

Yestertec Design Co.
P.O. Box 190
Center Valley, PA 18034
(610) 838-1194
(610) 838-1937 fax
www.yestertec.com
(kitchen workstations)

Yorktowne Cabinets
P.O. Box 231
Red Lion, PA 17356
(800) 777-0056
www.yorktowneinc.com

COUNTERTOPS

PORCELAIN
ENAMELED METAL

American Porcelain Enamel Co.
3506 Singleton Blvd
Dallas, TX 75212
(214) 637-4775
(214) 631-5424

Custom Ceramic Coatings, Inc.
419 Nashville Road
P.O. Box 105
Lenzburg, IL 62255
(618) 475-2710
(618) 475-4657 fax
www.CustomCeramic.com

TILE

American Marrazi Tile
359 Clay Road
Sunnyvale, TX 75182
(972) 226-0110
(972) 226-2263 fax
www.am-marazzi.com

Amsterdam Corp.
150 E. 58th Street
New York, NY 10155
(212) 644-1350
(213) 935-6291 fax

Art Tile
4336 Broadway
Oakland, CA 94611
(510) 547-8288

Brooklyn Tile Supply Corp.
184 - 4th Avenue
Brooklyn, NY 11217
(718) 875-1789
(718) 875-1791 fax

Classic Ceramic Tile
124 Tices Lane
E. Brunswick, NJ 08816
(800) 394-7770
(732) 238-2904 fax
www.classiccerramictile.com

Country Floors
15 E. 16th Street
New York, NY 10003
(212) 627-8300
(212) 627-7742 fax

Creative Tile Marketing
12323 SW 55th Street
Bldg #1000, #1010
Ft. Lauderdale, FL 33330
(954) 252-9989
(305) 858-9926 fax

Endicott Clay Products
57120 – 707 Road
Endicott, NE 68350
(402) 729-3315
(402) 729-5804 fax

Florida Tile Industries
P.O. Box 447
Lakeland, FL 33802
(941) 687-7171
(941) 284-4007
www.fltile.com

Daltile
7834 Hawn Fwy
P.O. Box 170130
Dallas, TX 75217
(800) 933-8453
(214) 309-4457 fax
www.daltile.com

Designs in Tile
Box 358-AB
Mt. Shasta, CA 96067
(530) 926-2629
www.designsintile.com

Fireclay Tile
495 W. Julian Street
San Jose, CA 95110
(408) 275-1182
(408) 275-1187 fax
www.fireclay.com

London Tile Co.
65 Walnut Street
New London, OH 44851
(419) 929-1551
(419) 929-1552 fax

McIntyre Tile Co.
55 W. Grant Street
Healdsburg, CA 95448
(707) 433-8866
(707) 433-0548 fax

Mission Tile West
853 Mission Street
South Pasadena, CA 91030
(818) 799-4595
(818) 799-8769 fax

Pratt and Larsen
1201 SE 3rd Avenue
Portland, OR 97214
(503) 231-9464

Red Clay Tile Works
75 Meade Avenue
Pittsburgh, PA 15202
(412) 734-2222

Renaissance Tile and Marble
P.O. Box 412
Cherry Valley, NY 13320
(607) 264-8474
(607) 267-8474 fax

Ann Sacks Tile and Stone
8120 NE 33rd
Portland, OR 97211
(503) 281-7751
(503) 287-8807 fax
www.annsaks.com

Seneca Tiles
7100 S. Country Road, Ste. 23
Attica, OH 44807
(800) 426-4335
(419) 426-1735 fax

Shep Brown Associates
24 Cummings Parkway
Woburn, MA 01801
(781) 935-8080
(617) 935-2090 fax

Summitville Tiles
P.O. Box 73
S.R. 644
Summitville, OH 43962
(330) 223-1511
(330) 223-1414 fax

Terra Designs Tileworks
49B Route 202 South
P.O. Box 41
Far Hills, NJ 07931
(908) 234-0440
(908) 781-1810 fax

Tile Restoration Center
3511 Interlake Avenue North
Seattle, WA 98103
(206) 633-4866
(206) 633-3489 fax

Tile Showcase
291 Arsenal Street
Watertown, MA 02472
(617) 926-1100
(617) 647-9934

Urban Archaeology
143 Franklin Street
New York, NY 10013
(212) 431-4646

U.S. Ceramic Tile Co.
10233 Sandyville Road SE
East Sparta, OH 44626
(330) 866-5531

Sherle Wagner Intl.
60 E. 57th Street
New York, NY 10022
(212) 758-3300
(212) 207-8010 fax
www.sherlewagner.com

STONE

Buckingham-Virginia Slate Corp.
P.O. Box 8
Arvonia, VA 23004
(804) 581-1131
(804) 581-1130 fax

Chiarini Marble and Stone
830 E. Washington Avenue
Santa Ana, CA 92701
(714) 547-5466
(714) 546-7282 fax
(soapstone)

Echeguren Slate
1495 Illinois Street
San Francisco, CA 94107
(800) 992-0701
(415) 206-9353 fax
www.echeguren.com

Fireslate 2
(800) 523-5902
www.fireslate.com

Ann Sacks Tile and Stone
(see Tile)

Sheldon Slate Products
38 Farm Quarry Road
Monson, ME 04464
(207) 997-3615
(207) 997-2966 fax
www.sheldonslate.com

Shep Brown Associates
(see Tile)

The Stone Yard
www.StoneyaRoad.com

Tile Showcase
(see Tile)

Vermont Soapstone
P.O. Box 268
248 Stoughton Pond Road
Perkinsville, VT 05151
(802) 263-5404
(803) 263-9451 fax

Vermont Structural Slate Co.
P.O. Box 98
3 Prospect Street
Fair Haven, VT 05743
(800) 343-1900
(802) 265-3865 fax
www.vermontstructuralslate.com

Waterworks
(see Tile)

WOOD

Aged Woods
2331 E. Market Street
York, PA 17402
(800) 233-9307
(717) 840-1468 fax
www.agedwoods.com

Albany Woodworks
(see Flooring)

Architectural Timber and Millwork
49 Mt. Warner Road
P.O. Box 719
Hadley, MA 01035
(413) 586-3045
(413) 586-3046 fax

Augusta Lumber Co.
(see Flooring)

Authentic Pine Floors
(see Flooring)

Authentic Wood Floors
(see Flooring)

Barnes Lumber Mfg.
(see Flooring)

Carlisle Restoration Lumber
Attn: Angela
1676 Route 9
Stoddard, NH 03464
(800) 595-9663
(603) 446-3540 fax
www.wideplankflooring.com

Centre Mills Antique Floors
(see Flooring)

Chestnut Specialists
400 Harwinton Avenue
Plymouth, CT 06782
(860) 283-4209
(860) 283-4209 fax
www.chestnutspec.com

Chestnut Woodworking and Antique Flooring Co.
(see Flooring)

M.L. Condon Co.
(see Flooring)

Craftsman Lumber Co.
436 Main Street
Groton, MA 01450
(978) 448-5621
(978) 448-2754 fax
www.craftsmanlumber.com

Duluth Timber Co.
P.O. Box 16717
Duluth, MN 55816
(218) 727-2145
(218) 727-0393 fax
www.duluthtimber.com

Forester Moulding and Lumber
(see Flooring)

Goodwin Heart Pine Co.
(see Flooring)

Granville Mfg. Co.
(see Flooring)

The Joinery Co.
(see Flooring)

Longwood Restoration
330 Midland Place, No. 3
Lexington. KY 40505
(606) 233-2268
(606) 299-8205 fax

Mountain Lumber Co.
P.O. Box 289
Ruckersville, VA 22968
(800) 445-2671
(804) 985-4105 fax
www.mountainlumber.com

New England Hardwood Supply
(see Flooring)

New England Wholesale Hardwoods
(see Flooring)

Patina Woods Co.
3563 New Franklin Road
Chambersburg, PA 17201
(717) 264-8009

Pioneer Millworks
1180 Commercial Drive
Farmington, NY 14425
(716) 924-9962
(716) 289-3221 fax
www.newenergyworks.com

Plaza Hardwood
(see Flooring)

Quality Woods Ltd.
63 Flanders Bartley Road
Lake Hiawatha, NJ 07034
(973) 584-7554
(973) 584-3875 fax

Rare Earth Hardwoods
(see Flooring)

River City Woodworks
825 Ninth Street
New Orleans, LA 70115
(800) 207-7738
(504) 899-7278

A.E. Sampson and Son
(see Flooring)

Timberknee Ltd.
Waterman Road
S. Royalton, VT 05068
(800) 720-9823

Timeless Wood
(see Flooring)

Woodhouse
(see Flooring)

The Woods Co.
(see Flooring)

World Class Floors
(see Flooring)

Yankee Exotic Woods
(see Flooring)

DECOR

CURTAINS

Arts and Crafts Period Textiles
Dianne Ayres
5427 Telegraph W2
Oakland, CA 94609
(510) 654-1645

J. R. Burrows and Co.
P.O. Box 522
Rockland, MA 02370
(800) 347-1795
www.burrows.com

Liberty Valances and Curtains
768 N. Fairoaks Avenue
Pasadena, CA 91103
(626) 395-9997
(626) 792-0636 fax
www.libertyvalances.com

London Lace
215 Newbury Street
Boston, MA 02116
(800) 926-5223
(617) 267-0770 fax
www.londonlace.com

Prairie Textiles
Ann Wallace and Friends
P.O. Box 2344
Venice, CA 90244
(213) 617-3310
www.webmonger.com/AnnWallace

United Crafts
127 West Putnam Avenue #123
Greenwich, CT 06830
(203) 869-4898
(203) 869-4470 fax

Vintage Valances
Box 43326
Cincinnati, OH 45243
(513) 561-8665
(513) 561-8665 fax

STENCILS

Helen Foster Stencils
71 Main Street
Sanford, ME 04073
(207) 490-2625

Trimbelle River Studios
Amy A. Miller
P.O. Box 568
Ellsworth, WI 54011
(715) 273-4844
www.trimbelleriver.com

DESIGNERS

Artistic License
P.O. Box 881841
San Francisco, CA 94188
(415) 675-9996
(crafts guild)

Ivy Hill Interiors
Laurie Taylor
3920 SW 109th Street
Seattle, WA 98146
(206) 243-6768
(interior design)

Karen Hovde, Interior Vision
23 Oakshore Court
Port Townsend, WA 98368
(888) 385-3161
(interior design)

**National Kitchen and Bath
Association**
(800) 843-6522
www.nkba.org
(referrals to Certified Kitchen
and Bath Designers)

Victorian Interiors
575 Hayes Street
San Francisco, CA 94102
(415) 431-7191
(415) 431-7144 fax
(interior design)

Marti Wachtel
1376 Yosemite Avenue
San Jose, CA 95126
(408) 998-2545
(408) 377-3555 fax
(interior design)

ELECTRICAL

Classic Accents
P.O. Box 1181
Southgate, MI 48195
(734) 941-8011
(734) 284-7185 fax
(push-button light switches)

FAUCETS, PLUMBING, SINKS

A-Ball Plumbing Supply
1703 W. Burnside
Portland, OR 97209
(800) 228-0134
(503) 228-0030 fax
www.a-ball.com

American Standard
One Centennial Avenue
Piscataway, NJ 08855
(800) 524-9797
www.americanstandard.com

Antique Baths and Kitchens
2220 Carlton Way
Santa Barbara, CA 93109
(805) 962-2598

Antique Hardware and Home
19 Buckingham Plantation Drive
Bluffton, SC 29910
(800) 422-9982
(843) 837-9790 fax

Bathroom Machineries
P.O. Box 1020
495 Main Street
Murphys, CA 95247
(800) 255-4426
(209) 728-2320 fax
www.deabath.com

Baths From The Past
83 E. Water Street
Rockland, MA 02370
(800) 697-3871

Burgess Intl. Inc.
6810 Metroplex
Romulus, MI 48174
(800) 837-0092
(800) 860-0093 fax
www.burgessinternational.com
www.homeportfolio.com
www.improvenet.com

Chicago Faucets
2100 S. Clearwater Drive
Des Plaines, IL 60018
(847) 803-5000
(847) 803-5454 fax

The Copper Sink Co.
P.O. Box 732
Los Olivos, CA 93441
(805) 693-0733

Delta Faucet
55 E. 11th Street
Indianapolis, IN 46280
(800) 345-3358
www.deltafaucet.com

**Do It UR Self Plumbing and
Heating Supply**
3100 Brighton Blvd
Denver, CO 80216
(303) 297-0455
(303) 295-0771 fax

Elkay
(630) 574-8484
www.elkay.com

**Gemini Bath and Kitchen
Products**
P.O. Box 43398
Tuscon, AZ 85733
(520) 770-0667
(520) 770-9964 fax
www.geminibkp.com

George's Plumbing
690 S. Fairoaks Avenue
Pasadena, CA 91106
(626) 792-5547

Gerber Plumbing Fixtures Corp.
4656 W. Touhy Avenue
Chicago, IL 60646
(800) 5-GERBER fax
(847) 675-5192 fax

German Silver Sink Co.
5754 Lodgewyck
Detroit, MI 48224
(313) 882-7730
(313) 882-7739 fax

Kohler
444 Highland Drive
Kohler, WI 53044
(414) 457-4441
(414) 459-1656 fax
www.kohlerco.com

Kolson
653 Middle Neck Road
Great Neck, NY 11023
(516) 487-1224
(516) 487-1231 fax
www.kolson.com

Mac the Antique Plumber
6325 Elvas Avenue
Sacramento, CA 95819
(800) 916-2284
(916) 454-4150 fax

Mansfield Plumbing Products
8425 Pulsar Place
Columbus, OH 43240
(614) 825-0960
(615) 825-0989 fax
www.mansfieldplumbing.com

Opella
4062 Kingston Court
Marietta, GA 30060
(800) 969-0339
(770) 955-5955 fax

The Renovator's Supply
P.O. Box 2515
Conway, NH 03818
(800) 659-2211

Restoration Works
9 St. Louis Place
Buffalo, NY 14202
(716) 856-6400
(716) 856-6401 fax
www.restoworks.com

Rohl LLC
1559 Sunland Lane
Costa Mesa, CA 92626
(714) 557-1933
(714) 557-8635 fax

The Sink Factory
2140 San Pablo Avenue
Berkeley, CA 94702
(510) 540-8193
www.sinkfactory.com

**Strom Plumbing by
Sign of the Crab**
3756 Omec Circle
Rancho Cordova, CA 95742
(916) 638-2722
(916) 638-2725 fax
www.signofthecrab.com

Sunrise Specialty Co.
5540 Doyle Street
Emeryville, CA 94608
(510) 654-1794

George Taylor Specialties
100 Hudson Street
Store B
New York, NY 10013
(212) 226-5369
(212) 274-9487 fax

Touch of Brass
9052 Chevolet Drive
Ellicott City, MD 21042
(800) 272-7734
(410) 750-7275 fax
www.atouchofbrass.com

Watercolors Inc.
Garrison, NY 10524
(914) 424-3327
(914) 424-3169 fax

Waterworks
(see Tile)

FLOORING

LINOLEUM

Forbo Industries
P.O. Box 667
Hazleton, PA 18201
(800) 342-0604
(570) 450-0258 fax
www.forbo-industries.com

Linoleum City
5657 Santa Monica Blvd
Hollywood, CA 90038
(323) 469-0063
(323) 465-5866 fax

TILE
(see Countertops)

VINYL

Amtico International
6480 Roswell Road
Atlanta, GA 30328
(404) 267-1900
(404) 267-1901
www.amtico.com

Armstrong World Industries
2500 Columbia Avenue
Lancaster, PA 17604
(800) 292-6308
www.armstrongfloors.com

Congoleum
3705 Quakerbridge Road, Ste. 211
Mercerville, NJ 08619
(609) 584-3000
(609) 584-3518 fax
www.congoleum.com

Mannington Mills
P.O. Box 30
Mannington Mills Road
Salem, NJ 08079
(800) 356-6787
(856) 339-6124
www.mannington.com

WOOD

Albany Woodworks
P.O. Box 729
Albany, LA 70711
(225) 567-1155
www.albanywoodworks.com

Augusta Lumber Co.
567 N. Charlotte Avenue
Waynesboro, VA 22980
(540) 946- 2841
(540) 946-9168 fax
www.comclin.net/augustalumber

Authentic Pine Floors
Sales: send info to Sharon
P.O. Box 206
4042 Hwy 42
Locust Grove, GA 30248
(800) 283-6038
(770) 914- 2925

Authentic Wood Floors
P.O. Box 153
Glen Rock, PA 17327
(717) 428-0904
(717) 428-0464 fax

Barnes Lumber Mfg.
P.O. Box 1383
Statesboro, GA 30459
(912) 764-8875
(912) 764-8713
www.barneslumber.com

Centre Mills Antique Floors
P.O. Box 16
Aspers, PA 17304
(717) 334-0249
(717) 334-6223 fax
www.igateway.com/mall/home-imp/wood/index

Chestnut Woodworking and Antique Flooring Co.
P.O. Box 204
West Cornwall, CT 06796
(860) 672-4300
(860) 672-2441 fax

M.L. Condon Co.
254 Ferris Avenue
White Plains, NY 10603
(914) 946-4111
(914) 946-3779 fax

Forester Moulding and Lumber
152 Hamilton Street
Leominster, MA 01453
(800) 649-9734
(978) 534-8356 fax
www.forestermoulding.com

Goodwin Heart Pine Co.
106 SW 109 Place
Micanopy, FL 32667
(352) 466-0339
(352) 466-0608 fax
www.heartpine.com

Granville Mfg. Co.
Rt.100
P.O. Box 15
Granville, VT 05747
(802) 767-4747
(802) 767-3107 fax
www.woodsiding.com

The Joinery Co.
P.O. Box 518
Tarboro, NC 27886
(252) 823-3306
(252) 823-0818 fax

Launstein Hardwoods
384 S. Every Road
Mason, MI 48854
(517) 676-1133

Linden Lumber
P.O. Drawer 480369
Hwy 43N
Linden, AL 36748
(334) 295-8751
(334) 295-8088 fax

Mayse Woodworking Co.
319 Richardson Road
Lansdale, PA 19446
(215) 822-8307
(215) 822-8307 fax

Millwork Designs
230 Topaz Lane
Washington C.H., OH 43160
(740) 335-5203

New England Hardwood Supply
P.O. Box 2254
100 Taylor Street
Littleton, MA 01460
(800) 540-8683

New England Wholesale Hardwoods
Route 82 South
Pine Plains, NY 12567
(518) 398-9663
(518) 398-9666 fax
www.floorings.com

Plaza Hardwood
Attn: Tony Fuge
219 W. Manhattan Avenue
Santa Fe, NM 87501
(800) 662-6306
(505) 992-3260
(505) 466-0456 fax

J. L. Powell and Co.
723 Pine Log Road
Whiteville, NC 28472
(800) 227-2007
(919) 642-3164 fax

Rare Earth Hardwoods
6778 E. Traverse Hwy
Traverse City, MI 49684
(800) 968-0074
(800) 968-0094 fax

Robbins Flooring
25 Whitney Drive, Ste. 106
Milford, OH 45150
(800) 733-3309
(513) 831-7712 fax
www.robbinsflooring.com

A. E. Sampson and Son
P.O. Box 1010
171 Camden Road
Warren, ME 04864
(207) 273-4000
(207) 273-4006

Simmen Wholesale Lumber
7641 Wilbur Way
Sacramento, CA 95828
(916) 689-9112

Timeless Wood
7230 Route 14
Irasburg, VT 05845
(888) 515-0886
(954) 421-8606 fax

Vintage Pine Co.
P.O. Box 85
Prospect, VA 23960
(804) 574-6531
(804) 574-2401 fax

The Woods Co.
5045 Kansas Avenue
Chambersburg, PA 17201
(717) 263-6524
(717) 263- 9346 fax

World Class Floors
333 SE Second Avenue
Portland, OR 97214
(800) 547-6634
(503) 736-2566 fax
www.contactintl.com

Yankee Exotic Woods
P.O. Box 211
Cornish, NH 03746
(603) 675-6206
(603) 675-6306 fax

GLASS

S.A. Bendheim Co.
61 Willett Street
Passaic, NJ 07055
(800) 221-7379
(201) 471-3475 fax
(restoration glass)

Blenko Glass Co.
Attn: Jane McMan
P.O. Box 67
Fairgrounds Road
Milton, WV 25541
(304) 743-9081
(304) 743-0547 fax
www.citynet.net/blenko

HARDWARE

Acorn Mfg.
457 School Street
Box 31
Mansfield, MA 02048
(800) 835-0121
(800) 372-2676 fax
www.acornmfg.com

Addkison Hardware Co.
126 E. Amite Street
P.O. Box 102
Jackson, MS 39205
(800) 821-2750
(601) 354-1916 fax
www.addkisonhardware.com

Affordable Antique Bath and More
333 Oak Street
P.O. Box 444
San Andreas, CA 95249
(888) 303-2284
(209) 754-4950 fax
www.bathandmore.com
(glass knobs)

Al Bar-Wilmette Platers
127 Green Bay Road
Wilmette, IL 60091
(847) 251-0187
(847) 251-0281 fax)
(hardware restoration)

American Home Supply
191 Lost Lake Lane
Campbell, CA 95008
(408) 246-1962

Antique Doorknob Publishing Co.
P.O. Box 2609
Woodinville, WA 98072
(425) 483-5848
(425) 483-5908 fax
(books about hardware, research archive)

Antique Hardware and Home
(see Faucets)

Architects and Heroes Interiors
1809 W. 35th Street
Austin, TX 78703
(512) 467-9393
www.knobshop.com

Ball and Ball
463 W. Lincoln Hwy
Exton, PA 19341
(610) 363-7330
(610) 363-7639 fax

Bathroom Machineries
(see Faucets)

Bauerware Cabinet Hardware
Attn: Nancy
3886 - 17th Street
San Francisco, CA 94114
(415) 864-3886
www.bauerware.com

Bona Decorative Hardware
3073 Madison Road
Cincinnati, OH 45209
(513) 321-7877
(513) 371-7877 fax

Canaan Distributors
20 Largo Park
Stamford, CT 06907
(800) 882-6226
(203) 348-3268 fax

A Carolina Craftsman
975 S. Avocado Street
Anaheim, CA 92805
(714) 776-7877
(714) 533-0894

Cirecast
1790 Yosemite Avenue
San Francisco, CA 94124
(415) 863-8319
(415) 863-7721

Crown City Hardware Co.
1047 N. Allen Avenue
Pasadena, CA 91104
(626) 794-1188
(626) 794-1439 fax
www.crowncityhardware.com

Decorative Hardware Studio
P.O. Box 627
Chappaqua, NY 10514
(914) 238-5251
(914) 230-4880 fax
www.decorative-hardware.com

Englewood Hardware Co.
25 N. Dean Street
Englewood, NJ 07631
(201) 568-1937
(603) 568-2243 fax

Eugenia's Antique Hardware
5370 Peachtree Road
Chamblee, GA 30341
(800) 337-1677
(770) 458-5966 fax
www.eugeniaantiquehardware.com
E-mail: eugeniashardware@ minespring.com

Grandpa Snazzy's Hardware
1832 S. Broadway
Denver, CO 80210
(303) 778-6508

Hardware Bath and More
20830 Coolidge Hwy
Oak Park, MI 48237
(248) 398-4560
(248) 546-2328 fax
www.h-b-m.com

Hinges and Handles
P.O. Box 103
100 Lincolnway East
Osceola, IN 46561
(800) 533-4782
(219) 674-8878
(219) 674-5767 fax

Horton Brasses
P.O. Box 95
Nooks Hill Road
Cromwell, CT 06416
(860) 635-4400
(860) 635-6473 fax
www.horton-brasses.com

Kayne and Son Custom Hardware
100 Daniel Ridge Road
Candler, NC 28715
(828) 667-8868
(828) 665-8303 fax

Phyllis Kennedy Hardware
10655 Andrade Drive
Zionsville, IN 46077
(317) 873-1316
(317) 873-8662 fax
(mfg. of parts for Hoosier cabinets)

Kolson
(see Faucets)

Liz's Antique Hardware
453 S. La Brea
Los Angles, CA 90036
(323) 939-4403
(323) 939-4387 fax
www.lahardware.com

Mac the Antique Plumber
(see Faucets)

Michigan Hoosier Co.
(see Cabinets)

Nostalgic Warehouse
701 E. Kingsley Road
Garland, TX 75041
(800) 522-7336
(972) 271-9726 fax
www.nostalgicwarehouse.com

Paxton Hardware
P.O. Box 256
Upper Falls, MD 21156
(800) 241-9741
(410) 592-2224 fax
www.paxtonhardware.com

The Renovator's Supply
(see Faucets)

Restoration Works
(see Faucets)

Touch of Brass
(see Faucets)

Van Dyke's Restorers
Fourth Avenue and Sixth Street
Woonsocket, SD 57385
(800) 558-1234
(604) 796-4085 fax
www.vandykes.com

Woodworker's Store
4365 Willow Drive
Medina, MN 55340
(612) 478-8201
(612) 478-8395 fax
www.woodworkerstore.com

HOUSE MUSEUMS AND HISTORIC SITES

The Adamson House
23200 Pacific Coast Hwy
P.O. Box 291
Malibu, CA 90265
(310) 456-8432

**Ardenwood Historic Farm
Patterson House**
34600 Ardenwood Blvd
Fremont, CA 94555
(510) 796-0663

The Biltmore Estate
One North Pack Square
Asheville, NC 28801
(800) 543-2961

Craftsman Farms
Attn: Susan Finkenberg,
museum shop manager
2352 Route 10 West
Morris Plains, NJ 07950
(973) 540-1165
www.parsippany.net/
craftsmanfarms.html

Dunsmuir Historic Estate
Attn: Debbie Bresso, gift
shop buyer
2960 Peralta Oaks Court
Oakland, CA 94605
(510) 615-5555
www.dunsmuir.org

**The Frank Lloyd Wright Home
and Studio**
951 Chicago Avenue
Oak Park, IL 60302
(708) 848-1500
www.wrightplus.org

The Gamble House
4 Westmoreland Place
Pasadena, CA 91103
(626) 793-3334

The Glessner House
1800 S. Prairie Avenue
Chicago, IL 60616
(312) 922-3432

**President Warren G. Harding
Home**
380 Mt. Vernon Avenue
Marion, OH 43302
(800) BUCKEYE

**Heritage Hill Historical Park
Bennett Ranch House**
25151 Serrano Road
Lake Forest, CA 92630
(949) 855-2028

Idaho State Historical Museum
610 N. Julia Davis Drive
Boise, ID 83702
(208) 334-2120

The Lanterman House
4420 Encinas Avenue
La Cañada–Flintridge, CA 91012
(818) 790-1421

Living History Farms
Attn: Karen Duis,
gift shop manager
2600 NW 11th Street
Urbandale, IA 50322
(515) 278-5286

The Marston House
3215 Seventh Avenue
San Diego, CA 92103
(619) 232-2654

The Rev. McKinney House
8369 University Avenue
La Mesa, CA 91941
(619) 466-0197

The Pleasant Home
217 S. Home Avenue
Oak Park, IL 60302
(708) 383-2654

The Purcell-Cutts House
2328 Lake Place
Minneapolis, MN 55405
(612) 870-3131
Notify: Jennifer
Minneapolis Institute of Art
2400 Third Avenue South
Minneapolis, MN 55404
(612) 870-3115

Riordan Mansion State Park
409 Riordan Road
Flagstaff, AZ 86001
(520) 779-4395

**The Harriet Beecher Stowe
House & Library**
77 Forest Street
Hartford, CT 06105
(860) 522-9258

Strong Museum
Attn: Christine Dettman,
shop manager
One Manhattan Square
Rochester, NY 14607
(716) 263-2700

LIGHTING

Aamsco Lighting
15-17 Brook Street
Jersey City, NJ 07302
(800) 221-9092
(201) 434-0722
(201) 434-8535 fax
www.aamsco.com
(reproduction Edison bulbs)

Ball and Ball
(see Hardware)

Bathroom Machineries
(see Faucets)

Brass Light Gallery
Attn: Wayne
131 S. First Street
Milwaukee, WI 53204
(800) 243-9595
(800) 505-9404 fax
(414) 271-7755 fax
www.brasslight.com

Brass Reproductions
9711 Canoga Avenue
Chatsworth, CA 91311
(818) 709-7844
(818) 709-5918 fax

Classic Illumination
2743 Ninth Street
Berkeley, CA 94710
(510) 849-1842
(510) 849-2328 fax
www.classicillumination.com

Ensler Lighting
1793 Solano Avenue
Berkeley, CA 94707
(510) 526-4385

Gaslight Time
Attn: Randy, manager
5 Plaza Street West
Brooklyn, NY 11217
(718) 789-7185
(718) 789-6185 fax

Historic Lighting
10341 Jewell Lake Court
Fenton, MI 48430
(810) 629-4934
(810) 629-5556 fax

Howard's Antique Lighting
203 Hillsdale Road
Route 23
South Egremont, MA 01258
(413) 528-1232
http://bcn.net/~1romla/
(restoration)

Kyp-Go
Attn: Elizabeth
526 Geneva Road
Glen Ellyn, IL 60137
(630) 942-8181
(630) 469-8121 fax
(reproduction Edison bulbs)

Kruesel's General Merchandise
Attn: John
22 Third Street SW
Rochester, MN 55902
(507) 289-8049
(507) 289-8602 fax

Liz's Antique Hardware
(see Hardware)

Nowell's Inc.
490 Gate 5 Road
P.O. Box 295
Sausalito, CA 94966
(415) 332-4933
(415) 332-4936 fax
www.nowell'sinc@aol.com

**Rejuvenation Lamp and
Fixture Co.**
2550 NW Nicolai Street
Portland, OR 97210
(888) 343-8548
(800) 526-7329 fax
www.rejuvenation.com

Restoration Works
(see Faucets)

Roy Electric Co.
22 Elm Street
Westfield, NJ 07090
(800) 366-3347
(908) 317-4629 fax
www.westfieldnj.com/roy

Ruiz Antique Lighting
2333 Clement Avenue
Alameda, CA 94501
(510) 769-6082
(510) 769-1374 fax

St. Louis Antique
Lighting Co.
Attn: Gary Behm
801 N. Skinker Blvd
St. Louis, MO 63130
(314) 863-1414
(314) 863-6702 fax

Things Deco
Attn: Bob Josen
130 E. 18th Street, Ste. 8F
New York, NY 10003
(212) 362-8961

Urban Archaeology
(see Countertops)

ORGANIZATIONS

Friends of Terra Cotta
771 West End Avenue, Ste. 10E
New York, NY 10025
(212) 932-1750
www.preserve.org

National Trust for Historic
Preservation
1785 Massachusetts Avenue NW
Washington, DC 20036
(202) 588-6000
(202) 588-6038 fax
www.nationaltrust.org

Tile Heritage Foundation
P.O. Box 1850
Healdsburg, CA 95448
(707) 431-TILE
(707) 431-8455 fax

PERIODICALS

American Bungalow
123 S. Baldwin Avenue
Sierra Madre, CA 91024
(800) 350-3363
(818) 355-1220 fax
www.ambungalow.com

Fine Homebuilding
Fine Woodworking
The Taunton Press
63 S. Main Street
P.O. Box 5506
Newtown, CT 06470
(203) 426-8171
www.finehomebuilding.com

Old House Interiors
2 Main Street
Gloucester, MA 01930
(978) 283-3200
www.oldhouseinteriors.com

Old House Journal
2 Main Street
Gloucester, MA 01930
(978) 283-3200
www.oldhousejournal.com

RESTORATION CONSULTANTS

Benriter Restoration
John Benriter
2300 Stonyvale Road
Tujunga, CA 91042
(818) 353-1136

Steven Ballew
1521 - 37th Street
Sacramento, CA 95816
(916) 455-5908

Paul Duchscherer
303 Roosevelt Way
San Francisco, CA 94114
(415) 861-6256

House Dressing
Jane Powell
P.O. Box 31683
Oakland, CA 94604
E-mail: hsedressng@aol.com

Restoration True
Norman Finnance
P.O. Box 90367
San Jose, CA 95109
(408) 910-6970

SALVAGE YARDS

Adkins Architectural Antiques
3515 Fannin Street
Houston, TX 77004
(713) 522-6547
www.adkinsantiques.com

American Salvage
9200 NW 27th Avenue
7001 NW 27th Avenue
Miami, FL 33147
(305) 691-7001
www.americansalvage.com

Antiquities & Oddities
Architectural Salvage
2045 Broadway
Kansas City, MO 64108
(816) 283-3740
(816) 842-4606

Architectural Accents
Attn: Charles
2711 Piedmont Road
Atlanta, GA 30305
(404) 266-8700

Architectural Antique and
Salvage Co. of Santa Barbara
726 Anacapa Street
Santa Barbara, CA 93101
(805) 965-2446

Architectural Antiques
607 Washington Avenue South
Minneapolis, MN 55415
(612) 332-8344
(612) 332-8967 fax
www.archantiques.com

Architectural Antiques
Exchange
715 N. Second Street
Philadelphia, PA 19123
(215) 922-3669

Architectural Antiquities
Harborside, ME 04642
(207) 326-4938

Architectural Artifacts
2207 Larimer Street
Denver, CO 80033
(303) 292-6812

Architectural Artifacts
4325 N. Ravenswood Avenue
Chicago, IL 60613
(773) 348-0622

Architectural Elements
818 E. Eighth Street
Sioux Falls, SD 57103
(605) 339-9646

Architectural Emporium
207 Adams Avenue
Canonsburg, PA 15317
(724) 746-4301

Architectural Salvage
5001 N. Colorado Blvd
Denver, CO 80204
(303) 615-5432

Architectural Salvage
103 W. Michigan
201 E. Michigan
Grass Lake, MI 49240
(517) 522-8715

Architectural Salvage
Warehouse
53 Main Street
Burlington, VT 05401
(802) 658-5011
www.architecturalsalvagevt.com

Architectural Salvage, W.D.
618 E. Broadway
Louisville, KY 40202
(502) 589-0670

Artefacts Architectural Antiques
P.O. Box 513
St. Jacobs, ON N0B 2N0
Canada
(519) 664-3760
www.artefactsaa.com

Bauer Bros.
2500 Elm Street
Minneapolis, MN 55414
(612) 331-9492

Berkeley Architectural Salvage
1167 - 65th Street
Oakland, CA 95608
(510) 655-2270

The Brass Knob
Attn: Donetta George
2311 - 18th Street NW
Washington, DC 20009
(202) 332-3370
www.washingtonpoStreetcom/
yp/brassknob

By-Gone Days Antiques
3100 South Blvd
Charlotte, NC 28209
(704) 527-8717
(704) 527-0232 fax
www.by-gonedays.com

Colonial Antiques
5000 W. 96th Street
Indianapolis, IN 46268
(317) 873-2727

Dick's Antiques
670 Lake Avenue
Bristol, CT 06010
(860) 584-2566
www.rsblaschkesnet.net

Governor's Antiques and
Architectural Materials
8000 Antique Lane
Mechanicsville, VA 23116
(804) 746-1030

Great Gatsbys
5070 Peachtree Industrial Blvd
Atlanta, GA 30341
(800) 428-7297

Historic York Inc.'s
Architectural Warehouse
224 N. George Street
York, PA 17401
(717) 854-7152

Kimberly's Old-House Gallery
1600 Jonquill Lane
Wausau, WI 54401
(715) 359-5077

Materials Unlimited
2 W. Michigan Avenue
Ypsilanti, MI 48197
(800) 299-9462
www.materialsunlimited.com

Morrow's
2784-B Jacksonville Hwy
Medford, OR 97501
(541) 770-6867

Myers Restoration and
Architectural Salvage
RFD 2, Box 1250
Clinton, ME 04927
(207) 453-7010

Off the Wall,
Architectural Antiques
P.O. Box 4561
Lincoln near Fifth
Carmel, CA 93921
(831) 624-6165
www.imperialearth.com/OTW/

Ohmega Salvage
2407 San Pablo Avenue & 2400
Berkeley, CA 94702
(510) 843-7368
(510) 843-7123 fax
www.ohmegasalvage.com

Old Home Supply
1801 College Avenue
Fort Worth, TX 76110
(817) 927-8004

The Old House Parts Co.
24 Blue Wave Mall
Kennebunk, ME 04043
(207) 985-1999
www.oldhouseparts.com

Olde Good Things
124 W. 24th Street
New York, NY 10011
(212) 989-8401
(212) 463-8005 fax
www.oldegoodthings.com

Brad Oliver Antiques
Box 303
Cresco, PA 18326
(570) 595-3443

Omega Too
2204 San Pablo Avenue
Berkeley, CA 94702
(510) 843-7123 fax
www.ohmegasalvage.com

Osceola Antiques
117 Cascade Street
Osceola, WI 54020
(715) 294-2886

Pinch of the Past
109 W. Broughton Street
Savannah, GA 31401
(912) 232-5563
www.pinchofthepast.com

Restoration Supply Co.
736 Walnut Street
Royersford, PA 19468
(610) 372-3137

Salvage Heaven, Inc.
6633 W. National Avenue
West Allis, WI 53214
(414) 329-7170
www.salvageheaven.com

Salvage One
1524 S. Sangamon Street
Chicago, IL 60608
(312) 733-0098
www.salvageone.com

Scavenger's Paradise
5453 Satsuma Avenue
North Hollywood, CA 91601
(323) 877-7945

Soll's Antiques
P.O. Box 307
Canaan, ME 04924
(207) 474-5396
www.antiquestainedglass.net

This and That
1701 Rumrill Blvd.
San Pablo, CA 94806
(510) 232-1273

United House Wrecking
535 Hope Street
Stamford, CT 06906
(203) 348-5371
www.united-antiques.com

Urban Archaeology
(see Countertops)

Vermont Salvage Exchange
P.O. Box 453
White River Junction, VT 05001
(802) 295-7616

VENTILATION

Broan/Nu-Tone Group
926 W. State Street
Hartford, WI 53027
(800) 558-1711
www.broan-nutone.com

Vent-A-Hood Co.
1000 N. Greenville
Richardson, TX 75083
(972) 235-5201
(972) 231-0663 fax
www.ventahood.com

WALLS

Charles Street Supply Co.
54 Charles Street
Boston, MA 02114
(800) 382-4360
(617) 367-0682 fax
(plaster washers)

Fastenation
P.O. Box 520068
Winthrop, MA 02152
(617) 846-6444
(617) 539-0534 fax
(plaster washers)

WEBSITES

Craftsman Home Connection
www.crafthome.com

RestorationCentral
www.restorationcentral.com

The Toaster Museum
www.antiquetoaster.com

WINDOWS

Adams Architectural Wood
Products
300 Trails Road
Eldridge, IA 52748
(319) 285-8000
(319) 285-8003 fax
www.adamsarch.com

Allegheny Restoration
P.O. Box 18032
Morgantown, WV 26507
(304) 594-2570
(304) 594-2810 fax
www.allegheny-restoration.com

Andersen Corp.
100 - 4th Avenue North
Bayport, MN 55003
(800) 426-4261
www.andersenwindows.com

Architectural Components
26 N. Leverett Road
Montague, MA 01351
(413) 367-9441
(413) 367-9461 fax

Architectural Detail in Wood
41 Parker Road
Shirley, MA 01464
(978) 425-9026
(978) 425-9028 fax

J. S. Benson Woodworking and
Design Co.
26 Birge Street
Brattleboro, VT 05301
(802) 254-3515
(802) 254-4874 fax

Marion H. Campbell
(see Cabinetry)

Copper Beech Millwork
30 Industrial Dr.
Northhampton, MA 01061
(800) 532-9110
(413) 582-0164 fax
www.copperbeech.com

Crestline Windows and Doors
888 Southview Drive
Mosinee, WI 54455
(715) 693-7000
(715) 693-8409 fax
www.crestlineonline.com

Drums Sash and Door Co.
P.O. Box 207
Drums, PA 18222
(570) 788-1145
(570) 788-3007 fax

Eagle Window and Door
375 E. Ninth Street
Dubuque, IA 52004
(319) 556-2270
(319) 556-4408 fax
www.eaglewindow.com

Eton Architectural Millwork
1210 Morse Avenue
Royal Oak, MI 48067
(248) 543-9100
(248) 543-7506 fax

Fine Woodworking Co.
16750 White Store Road
Boyds, MD 20841
(301) 972-8808
(301) 916-3509 fax

L. H. Hobein and Son
759 Snelson Road
Marshall, NC 28753
(828) 649-3238 ph/fax

Holtzer and Fenestra LLC
233 Butler Street
Brooklyn, NY 11217
(718) 254-0858
(718) 254-0858 fax

Hornspier Millwork
1690 S. Lake Michigan Drive
Sturgeon Bay, WI 54235
(920) 743-8823
(920) 743-8823 fax

Kolbe and Kolbe Millwork
1323 S. 11th Avenue
Wausau, WI 54401
(800) 955-8177
(715) 845-8270 fax
www.kolbe-kolbe.com

Lititz Planing Mill
302 E. Front Street
Lititz, PA 17543
(717) 626-2186
(717)626-0924 fax

Littleton Millwork
44 Lafayette Avenue
Littleton, NH 03561
(603) 444-2677
(603) 444-1056 fax

Millwork Supply Co.
2225 First Avenue South
Seattle, WA 98134
(206) 622-1450
(206) 292-9176 fax
www.millworksupply.com

J. P Moriarty Millwork
22 Clifton Street
Somerville, MA 02144
(617) 628-3000

Oakwood Classic and Custom Woodworks, Ltd.
517 W. Commercial Street
East Rochester, NY 14445
(716) 381-6009
(716) 383-8053 fax
www.oakwoodww.com

Peachtree Doors and Windows
4350 Peachtree Industrial Blvd
Norcrosss, GA 30071
(800) PEACH99
www.peach99.com

Pella Corp.
102 Main Street
Pella, IA 50219
(800) 84-PELLA
(515) 628-6457 fax
www.pella.com

Pozzi Windows
P.O. Box 5249
Bend, OR 97708
(541) 382-4411
(541) 385-3278 fax
www.pozzi.com

Rails and Stiles
145 Cherokee Trail
Indian Springs, AL 35124
(205) 967-2662
(205) 967-2662 fax

Restoration Supply Co.
842 N. Second Street
Redding, PA 19601
(610) 372-3137

Seekircher Steel Window Repair
2 Weaver Street
Scarsdale, NY 10583
(914) 725-1904
(914) 725-1122 fax
www.atsrc.com/des-site/
seekirch.htm

Semling-Menke Co.
P.O. Box 378
Merrill, WI 54452
(800) 333-2206
(715) 536-3067
www.semcowindows.com

Versatile Sash and Woodwork
1420 SE Water Avenue
Portland, OR 97214
(503) 238-6403
(503) 238-0669 fax

Weather Shield Windows and Doors
1 Weather Shield Plaza
Medford, WI 54451
(800) 477-6808
(715) 748-0169 fax
www.weathershield.com

Wicks Custom Woods
1100 Fifth Street
Highland, IL 62249
(618) 654-2191
(618) 654-3770 fax
www.wicks.com

Windsor Windows & Doors
Attn: Kris Winter @
  (515) 223-6660
900 S. 19th Street
West Des Moines, IA 50265
(800) 218-6186
(515) 226-8935 fax
www.windsorwindows.com

Wood Window Workshop
839 Broad Street
Utica, NY 13501
(315) 732-6755
(315) 733-0933 fax

Woodstone Co.
P.O. Box 223
Patch Road
Westminster, VT 05158
(802) 722-9217
(802) 722-9528 fax
www.woodstone.com

Woodwright Co.
P.O. Box 494
2091 Main Street
Brewster, MA 02631
(508) 896-3393

Zeluck Architectural Wood Windows and Doors
5300 Kings Hwy
Brooklyn, NY 11234
(800) 233-0101
(718) 531-2564 fax

BIBLIOGRAPHY

"When you steal one person's written words, that's plagiarism. When you steal a lot of people's written words, that's research."—Author Unknown

Beecher, Catherine, and Harriet Beecher Stowe. *American Woman's Home*. New York: J.B. Ford and Co., 1869. Reprint: New Brunswick, New Jersey: Rutgers University Press, 1998.

Duchscherer, Paul, and Douglas Keister. *The Bungalow, America's Arts and Crafts Home*. New York: Penguin Books, 1995.

———. *Inside the Bungalow, America's Arts & Crafts Interior*. New York: Penguin Books, 1997.

Franklin, Linda Campbell. *300 Years of Kitchen Collectibles*. Iola, Wisconsin: Krause Publications, 1997.

Hoosier Manufacturing Co. *The Kitchen Plan Book*. Newcastle, Indiana: Hoosier Manufacturing Co., 1917. Reprint by Sierra Madre, California: American Bungalow Magazine, 1995.

Jester, Thomas C. *Twentieth Century Building Materials*. Washington, D.C.: McGraw-Hill Companies, 1995.

Morgan. *Building with Assurance*. Chicago, 1921. Reprint as *Homes and Interiors of the 1920s*. Ottawa, Ontario: Lee Valley Tools, 1987.

National Trust for Historic Preservation. *The Well-Appointed Bath*. Washington, D.C.: The Preservation Press, 1989.

Old House Journal. *1999 Restoration Directory*. Washington, D.C.: Hanley-Wood, Inc., 1999.

Plante, Ellen M. *The American Kitchen, 1700 to the Present*. New York: Facts On File, Inc., 1995.

Prentice, Helaine Kaplan and Blair, and City of Oakland Planning Department. *Rehab Right*. Oakland, California: City of Oakland, 1978. Reprint by Berkeley, California: Ten Speed Press, 1986.

Makinson, Randell L. *Greene and Greene: The Passion and the Legacy*. Salt Lake City: Gibbs Smith, Publisher, 1998.

Smith, Bruce, and Alexander Vertikoff. *Greene and Greene Masterworks*. San Francisco: Chronicle Books, 1998.

Wilson, Henry L. *A Short Sketch of the Evolution of the Bungalow: From Its Primitive Crudeness to Its Present State of Artistic Beauty and Cozy Convenience*. Los Angeles, n.d. Reprint by Mineola, New York: Dover Publications, 1993.